Creating Contexts

Writing Introductions across Genres

CHRISTINE B. FEAK
JOHN M. SWALES

VOLUME 3 OF THE REVISED AND EXPANDED EDITION OF
English in Today's Research World

 The Michigan Series in English for
Academic & Professional Purposes

ISBN: 978-0-472-03456-7

2014   2013   2012   2011   4   3   2   1

Acknowledgments

This small collection of materials would not exist were if not for the input and support of others. We must begin by acknowledging the students enrolled in our academic writing courses. Students from all five levels of writing coursework offered by the English Language Institute have given us feedback that reflects the needs and understanding of the least to most experienced graduate students at the University of Michigan. Increasingly, our student population includes domestic students who see the value in our approach to teaching academic writing. We are grateful to all of our students who are always willing to let us use their writing as a source of insight and inspiration.

Beyond our classrooms, we have also had the opportunity to experiment with the materials in academic writing workshops sponsored by the graduate schools at the University of Michigan and the University of Maryland, College Park. Our workshops with the Presidential Scholars at the University of Michigan African Studies Center have also allowed us to receive feedback from academics who are farther along in their careers. Opportunities to work with our materials in the various workshop settings have been invaluable, reminding us that such teaching venues should not be ignored in the preparation of this and our other volumes.

A volume such as this requires a lot of work that is not directly related to materials development or the actual composing process. For this behind-the-scenes work, we would like to thank Kelly Lockman, who carried out an analysis of introductions of papers in the Michigan Corpus of Upper-level Students Papers (MICUSP). We again owe a debt of gratitude to our assistant, Vera Irwin, who took care of the tedious task of obtaining the permissions to use copyrighted material and was involved in other aspects of preparing this volume. While the permission process is often straightforward, this has not always been the case for us. Vera's persistence and creativity in this matter have been nothing less than superb. We also very much appreciate Vera's contribution to the online commentary and her insightful feedback on our material as it evolved.

Discussions with colleagues also helped shape the final form of this work.

We express our thanks to Dr. Jason Lim for not only sharing his unpublished research with us, but for the lively discussion regarding the CaRS model and his alternative views on moves. Discussions with our fellow ELI instructors, especially Mindy Matice, were also extremely valuable in that they revealed how others use and re-purpose the tasks.

The anonymous reviewers also gave us extremely helpful feedback. While we were not always able to incorporate their suggestions in this volume, we did carefully consider their observations and revise the work to the extent that this was possible. We particularly appreciated the thoughtful comments that revealed something of the reviewers' teaching contexts and student demographics, again reminding us that we always need to look beyond our own teaching environment. We also need to acknowledge the informal feedback that our editor, Kelly Sippell, receives from users of our materials and sometimes solicits during her many conference trips. This informal feedback helps us respond to the needs of instructors elsewhere and has had a significant influence on the writing of this volume. We thank Kelly for being our intermediary. More important, during the writing of this volume, Kelly was her usual patient, supportive self. We know that she was hoping we would finish this volume much sooner than we did; we appreciate her understanding of our busy schedules and competing demands. Over the years, Kelly has been an outstanding editor, who is willing to give us considerable freedom in our projects, but not hesitant to nudge us in a certain direction. Her editorial expertise and knowledge of English for Academic Purposes have greatly contributed to our work. We continue to sing her praises whenever we are asked about publishing with the University of Michigan Press.

On a more personal level, Chris would like to say thank you again to Glen, who often seems more excited about her many projects than she is and more than willing to put up with the concomitant chaos. She would also like to say thanks to Karl and Angie, who, as university students, now understand and appreciate what she does, as well as show a genuine interest by checking on her progress. They proudly display her books and even use them to support their own writing, giving her a great sense of accomplishment. John again expresses his thanks to his longtime partner, Vi Benner, for her forbearance during the process of working on "yet another" book-length project.

CBF and JMS
Ann Arbor
January 2011

Grateful acknowledgment is given to the following authors, publishers, and individuals for permission to reprint copyrighted material.

Advances in Consumer Research for "Forget the 'real' thing—Take a copy! An explanatory model for the volitional purchase of counterfeit products" by Elfriede Penz and Barbara Stottinger, Vol. 32, 2005.

Annals of Pharmacotherapy for book review of "Miracle Medicines: Seven Lifesaving Drugs and the People who Created Them" by Robert L. Shook. Vol. 41, No. 7, pp. 1322–1323.

Applied Physics Letters for "Nucleation and growth of nickel nanoclusters of grapheme Moire on Rh(111)" by M. Sicot, O. Bouvron, U. Rudiger, Yu S. Dedkov, and M. Fonin, 96, 093115, 2010.

Computer Science for "Efficient model checking of applications with input/output," Vol. 4739/2007.

Earthquake Engineering Research Institute for excerpts from book review of *Dynamic Structures—Theory and Applications to Earthquake Engineering,* 3d ed., by Anil K. Chopra, reviewed by Farzad Naeim, *Earthquake Spectra,* Vol. 23, Issue 2, pp. 491–492.

Eastern Economic Journal for "The next great globalization: How disadvantaged nationsl can harness their financial systems to get rich" by Eva Marikova Leeds, Jan. 1, 2008.

Harold Ester for the sandhill crane illustration.

Flavour and Fragrance for "Analysis of honeydew melon flavor and GC-MS/MS identification (E,Z)-2,6-nonadienyl acetate" by Patrick L. Perry, Ying Wang, and Jianming Lin, Vol. 24, Issue 6, pp. 277–363.

Ronald F. Hoffman for three paragraphs from *Michigan Birds and Natural History* (late autumn population of sandhill cranes in Michigan).

Innovative Higher Education for "When topics are controversial: Is it better to discuss them face-to-face or online?" Vol. 31, No. 3, Oct. 2006.

Journal of Broadcasting & Electronic Media for "An exploratory study of reality appeal: Uses and gratifications of reality TV shows" by Zizi Papacharissi and Andrew L. Mendelson, Dec. 7, 2007, Vol. 51, Issue 2, pp. 355–370.

Journal of Empirical Finance for "Herding and information based trading" by Rhea Tingyu Zhou and Rose Neng Lai, June 2009, Vol. 16, No. 3.

Journal of General Internal Medicine for "Should physicians have facial piercings?" Vol. 20, No. 3, March 2005.

Journal of Law & Policy for "Adjudicating the right of publicity in three easy steps" by David Schlachter.

Journal of Marketing Research for "Why do consumers buy counterfeit luxury brands," Apr. 2009, Vol. 46, page 247.

Journal of Optics A: Pure and Applied Optics for introduction to "Intracavity frequency doubling of an InGaAs diode laser passively Q—switched with GaAs saturable absorber," Vol. 11, No. 10.

Journal of Visual Culture for "The terrain of the long take" by Laura Kissel, 2008, 7: 349–361.

Greta L. Krapohl for the use of her background section and selected feedback from her NRSA proposal. Used with permission.

Learning and Individual Differences for "Self-confidence and metacognitive processes" by Sabina Kleitman and Lazar Stankov, 2nd quarter 2007, Vol. 17, No. 2.

Marijke Leliveld for the excerpt from her dissertation "Ethics in Economic Decision-Making."

Tze-Hsiang (Stan) Liu for his introduction to "Personal Information Management."

Lithuanian Journal of Physics for "Investigation of dynamic characteristics of InGaAsP/InP Lase Diodes," Vol. 46, No. 1, 2006, pp. 33–38.

Min-Seok Pang for his review of "Co-creation of value in a platform ecosystem."

Scientometrics for "The efficiency of self-citations in economics," April 1, 2006.

Solid State Electronics Journal for "Electrical characteristics of GaAs nanocrystalline thin film" by J. Nayak and S. N. Sahu, Vol. 50, No. 2, February 2006.

Ping Yu for her Web 2.0 paper introduction.

Every effort has been made to contact the copyright holders for permission to reprint borrowed material. We regret any oversights that may have occurred and will rectify them in future printings of this volume.

Contents

General Introduction to the Volumes

John and Chris first started putting together the book that became *English in Today's Research World: A Writing Guide (ETRW)* in early 1998. The book was largely based on teaching materials we had been developing through the 1990s for our advanced courses in dissertation writing and writing for publication at the University of Michigan. Ten years later, that "research world" and our understanding of its texts and discourses have both changed considerably. This revised and expanded series is an attempt to respond to those changes. It also attempts to respond to reactions to *ETRW* that have come from instructors and users and that have reached us directly, or through Kelly Sippell, ESL editor for the University of Michigan Press. One consistent feature of these comments has been that *ETRW* is somewhat unwieldy because it contains too many disparate topics. For the second edition, therefore, we have made the radical decision to break the original book into several small separate volumes, each of which offers an in-depth focus on a particular facet of academic writing. We hope in this way that instructors or independent researcher-users can choose those volumes that are most directly relevant to their own situations at any particular time.

However, we do need to stress that many of the genres we separately deal with are interconnected. Abstracts are always abstracts of some larger text. A conference talk may be based on a dissertation chapter, and may end up as an article. Grant proposals lead to technical reports, to dissertations, and to further grant proposals. A revised version of the diagram (see Figure 1) we used in *ETRW* in order to indicate these interconnected networks is even more relevant to this multivolume series.

One continuing development in the research world has been the increasing predominance of English as the vehicle for communicating research findings. Of late, this trend has been reinforced by policy decisions made by ministries of higher education, universities, and research centers that researchers and scholars will primarily receive credit for publications appearing in English-medium international journals, especially those that are included in the ISI database. Indeed, in recent years, the range of "acceptable" outlets has often further narrowed to those ISI journals that have a

Figure 1. Open and Supporting Academic Genres

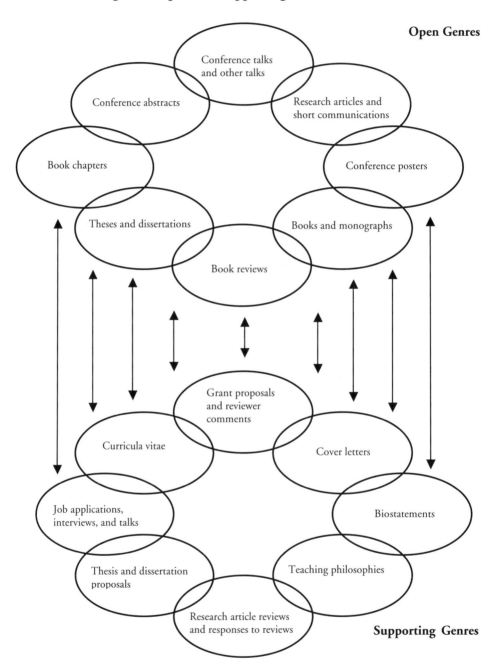

high impact factor (i.e., those with numerous citations to articles published over the previous three years). Selected countries around the world that have apparently adopted this kind of policy include Spain, the United Kingdom, China, Brazil, Malaysia, Chile, and Sri Lanka. Competition to publish in these high-status restricted outlets is obviously increasingly tough, and the pressures on academics to publish therein are often unreasonable. A further complicating development has been the rise and spread of the so-called "article-compilation" PhD thesis or dissertation in which the candidate is expected to have an article or two published in international journals *before* graduation.

The increasing numbers of people in today's Anglophone research world who do not have English as their first language has meant that the traditional distinction between native speakers and non-native speakers of English is collapsing. A number of scholars have rightly argued that we need to get rid of this discriminatory division and replace NNS by speakers of English as a *lingua franca* (ELF), English as an International Language (EIL), or speakers of English as an *additional language* (EAL). Today, the more valid and valuable distinctions are between senior researchers and junior researchers, on the one hand, and between those who have a broad proficiency in research English across the four skills of reading, writing, listening, and speaking and those with a narrow proficiency largely restricted to the written mode, on the other.

There have also been important developments in English for Academic Purposes and allied fields. The relevant journals have been full of articles analyzing research English, often discussing as well the pedagogical consequences of such studies. This has been particularly true of studies emanating from Spain. Indeed, the first international conference on "Publishing and presenting research internationally" was held in January 2007 at La Laguna University in the Canary Islands.

The use of corpus linguistic techniques applied to specialized electronic databases or corpora has been on the rise. The number of specialized courses and workshops has greatly expanded, partly as a way of utilizing this new knowledge, but more significantly as a response to the increasing demand. Finally, information is much more widely available on the Internet about academic and research English, particularly via search engines, such as Google Scholar. As is our custom, we have made much use of relevant research findings in these volumes, and we—and our occasional research assistants—have undertaken discoursal studies when we found gaps in the research literature. In this process we have also made use of a number of specialized corpora, including Ken Hyland's corpus of 240 research articles spread across eight disciplines and three others we have constructed at the University of Michigan—one of dental research articles, one of research articles from perinatology, and the Michigan Corpus of Upper-level Students Papers (MICUSP), which is available on the Internet at http://micusp.elicorpora.info/.

In this new venture, we have revised—often extensively—material from the original textbook, deleting texts and activities that we feel do not work so well, and adding much new material, at least partly in response to the developments mentioned earlier in this introduction. One concept, however, that we have retained from our previous textbooks is that of Language Focus sections, since these provide in-depth examinations of specific language options at what seem particularly appropriate points. As the volumes are published, we are interested in feedback from users and so we welcome comments at either or both cfeak@umich.edu or jmswales@umich.edu.

Introduction to the Introductions Volume

The writing of an introduction to a volume on introductions certainly gives us pause. There is indeed a bit of irony in writing the very kind of text that is the focus of this volume. Even so, we offer here a few thoughts, the writing of which we have left as our final task so that we could take a step back and look at how the materials in this volume actually turned out—in keeping with the first and last comments in Task One on pages 1–2.

In this volume, we have taken our usual genre-based approach with a strong emphasis on rhetorical consciousness-raising. Wherever possible, we have incorporated findings from research to support our views and strengthen the tasks. It is, however, important to note that the published research on introductions has been disproportionally aimed at published articles. Much less is known about introductions for other genres such as dissertations or proposals. Even when research is available, there are sometimes conflicting findings, as in the work on citations in dissertations. Where research is lacking, in order to support our claims and tasks we have done some small studies of introductions ourselves using our students' texts, the Michigan Corpus of Upper-level Students Papers (MICUSP), and texts available in journals and on the Internet. Despite our efforts in this regard, more research on introductions beyond those of research articles (RAs) is needed. This is particularly true when we consider that research is increasingly a multi- and interdisciplinary endeavor and that there may be no single best way to write an introduction in such circumstances. Thus, when uncertainties and conflicting ideas do arise while working through this volume, students, instructors, and independent users will need to do some analysis of the language and discourse practices of the fields of their particular interest.

The material presented in this volume is appropriate for graduate students and others already working in their chosen academic fields. The material has, in fact, been used with each of these groups in both writing courses and writing workshops. We believe that the material would also be suitable for those wishing to pursue a course of self-study. To target these different possible uses, we have included a variety of topics and tasks that we hope will deepen users' understanding of how to create a writing context for their work. Tasks range from evaluating text commentaries to open-ended questions and have been designed to generate lively classroom or workshop discussion as well as thoughtful consideration by an individual user.

As with all of our other volumes, in creating this volume we have envisioned instructors who have fairly extensive EAP teaching experience. We expect that this experience will enable teachers to supplement the material to target the needs of students in classes or in workshops. Teaching priorities and aims will be shaped by a variety of factors, such as whether one is teaching in the U.S. or another country, in a classroom with students who speak English as a first or an additional language, or in a classroom consisting of a multi- or single disciplinary group. Thus, there is no need to work through the topics in the volume in the order given or to cover all of them. For instance, some instructors may find it more useful to start with proposal introductions before research article introductions. Another way to address specific aims is by changing the sample texts in the volume, which come from a range of disciplines. We believe that including work from a variety of disciplines is a strength since this allows instructors, students, and independent users of the volume to consider alternative ways of writing. Comparisons of students' own work with that from other disciplines can be quite enlightening since these comparisons not only suggest other approaches to writing, but can reveal that concerns about language choice, discourse, and rhetoric are common to all writers, regardless of field, first language, or experience. If instructors and students do, however, want or need to focus on writing within a specific discipline, the relatively easy access to articles on the Internet through Google Scholar or publisher databases makes this possible. In many cases, the questions that accompany the sample texts in this volume can be used as is or slightly modified for use with introductions from any discipline. Some support for this latter activity is available in the Online Commentary available to users of this volume. This commentary provides answers for all of the tasks where this is possible. It also contains some teaching advice and further insights into the tasks, which we hope reveal more of the thinking behind the sections and activities.

The choice of content for this volume was rather straightforward in many respects. Of course, no teaching materials focusing on introductions would be complete without the now well-known CaRS model, which was first introduced in John's groundbreaking *Aspects of Article Introductions*[1] in 1981, further refined in *Genre Analysis*, and again revisited in *Research Genres* and which inspired other scholars to carry out their own research to either fine-tune the model for a particular discipline or perhaps dispute its relevance. Indeed, rightly or wrongly, as one might expect, RA introductions are central to this volume. Rather than suggesting that the CaRS model is the writing goal, however, we offer it as a starting point for RA authors, encouraging them to shape their introductions in light of practices within their own disciplines and the constraints of their research areas.

Beyond the emphasis on the RA introductions, we have also focused on introductions for other kinds of texts that are part of the graduate student writing experience, such as course papers in general and, more specifically, critiques, proposals, and dissertations. We are aware that many of our students have writing needs other than writing for publication and an exclusive emphasis on the latter would be inappropriate. Interestingly, in contrast to the abundance of research on RA introductions, rather less has been written on the introductions to these other genres and pedagogical genres. Thus, to further our understanding of these texts, we were fortunate to be able to turn to the MICUSP. This collection of student written papers includes 830 papers and more than 2.3 million words of running text written in a range of disciplines within the Humanities and Arts, Social Sciences, Biological and Health Sciences, and Physical Sciences at the University of Michigan. Each of the papers received the top grade of A. We also relied heavily on the work of our students in our writing classes, particularly those in ELI 420, Research Paper Writing, and in ELI 620 and 621, Dissertation Writing and Writing for Publication. The availability of these texts allowed our efforts on this volume to be data-driven, even in the absence of published research.

Finally, we welcome any feedback instructors would be willing to share with us. To strengthen the teaching advice portion of the Commentary, for instance, we would be very interested in learning how others have used the tasks or what tasks worked particularly well (or not) with a student group. Feel free to contact us with any observations that could improve this volume and better meet the needs of academic writers.

Creating Context is supported by an Online Commnetary at www.press. umich.edu/esl/compsite/ETRW/.

---

[1] To be reissued by the University of Michigan Press in 2011.

Some Preliminary Considerations

The beginning is half of the whole.

—Plato

When to Write the Introduction

When asked which part of a paper is the most difficult to write, many academic writers will point to the introduction. Whether writers are mainly engaged in producing course papers, papers for publication, or a dissertation, finding just the right context or backdrop for the work to be presented is a challenging task, so much so that many authors write the introduction only after much of a paper has been completed.

Task One

Consider these statements about approaches to writing an introduction. With which do you agree (A) or disagree (D)? Mark those about which you are unsure with a question mark (?). Work with a partner if you have one.

_____ 1. I don't yet know what my findings and conclusions will be, so there's no point in writing the introduction first.

_____ 2. Drafting the introduction gets me thinking about the shape of the paper as a whole, so that's why I write it first.

_____ 3. The introduction is so challenging, so it's best to leave it till later.

_____ 4. The introduction is the hardest part. If I can do that, I can do the rest. So, it's best to begin with it.

_____ 5. Writing the introduction first forces me to carefully consider the previous literature on the topic, and that's valuable.

_____ 6. The important parts are my own procedures and findings; I can always work on the introduction and previous literature later.

_____ 7. I need to have an introduction before I write any other part. Even a bad introduction is better than none at all.

_____ 8. It's best for me to wait and write the introduction last. If I write it first, it's really hard for me to critically evaluate and/or delete what I have done. So, I might just be wasting time if I try to write the intro first.

It is often argued that the introduction can determine whether your paper will be read or not—that you have to "catch the reader's interest" and "draw your reader into your paper." This may be important advice for an undergraduate composition course where you may be evaluated on how interesting the introduction is. This may also be true to some extent for published work; however, for many course papers, you have a captive audience. Your professor will read your paper no matter how engaging the introduction (at least this should be the case). This is *not* to say that you should not put some effort into your introduction for a course paper. After all, first impressions of your work do matter. What we are saying is, rather than worrying excessively about whether you have hooked your reader into your paper, your effort might be better spent on giving the impression that you are *engaged* in your topic and that you will have something *relevant* to say. As one of our students recently said, "You want your introduction to evoke a positive reaction to your work. You don't want your reader to think *so what* or *who cares.*" What this means is that your introduction should provide a context in which your reason for exploring your topic is apparent and in which your topic appears to be worth pursuing. This, we believe, is reasonable for most papers you are writing. So, how do you demonstrate that you have something interesting to say?

The Overall Shape of an Introduction

Many introductions can be described as having the shape of tapered glass with a base in which information is presented in order from general statements to more specific ones and concluding with a more general statement of the purpose or aims of the paper (Fig. 2). See pages 96–98 for a discussion of exceptions to this generalization. This may be accomplished within one paragraph or may require several paragraphs, depending on the type of text you are writing, the length of your text, and your topic.

Figure 2. General to Specific Shape of an Introduction

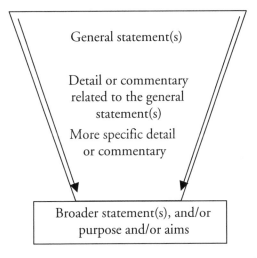

The information that you use to "fill the glass," so to speak, will vary in terms of what you are writing. For instance, the detail provided in a research paper for publication or a proposal will often consist of attempts to establish the research territory via a review of literature relevant to the topic at hand. For a course paper, the detail may serve to highlight a problem, clarify concepts, introduce solutions to a problem, or perhaps deal with a real-world issue as opposed to a research issue.

Task Two

Consider this introduction to a Communications course paper entitled "Shaping Public Opinion in the Web 2.0 Era" and written by a first-year graduate student, Ping Yu. Answer the questions on page 5. Sentence numbers have been added for ease of analysis.

> *A new medium is never an addition to an old one, nor does it leave the old one in peace. It never ceases to oppress the older media until it finds new shapes and positions for them.*
>
> —Marshall McLuhan

① In the late 20th century, research on the effects of the mass media consistently showed that the prominence of the issues presented in the news media was a central predictor of public opinion on the importance of those issues (Kiousis & McDevitt, 2009). ② Although this was true when the number of news sources was limited to newspapers and television, today the more likely source of news is the Internet, which offers users more control over the news content they access. ③ Indeed, according to Tim O'Reilly, we are in the "Web 2.0" period of the Internet era, in which we are influenced by social networking sites (Facebook and MySpace), online video sharing (YouTube), as well as online news sharing sites (Digg). ④ One of the key differences between Web 2.0 and the previous Web 1.0 era is that in the Web 1.0 period most users were simply acting as consumers of content, while now any participant can be a content creator in Web 2.0 due to the many technological aids designed to maximize the potential to produce content (Cormode & Krishnamurthy, 2008). ⑤ Since Internet users are now empowered to be either creators or selectors of content, there has been ongoing debate as to whether traditional news media still have the power to strongly shape public opinion.

⑥ To explore this issue, this paper examines the overlap and divergence of news content on two sets of news sources representing different media. ⑦ One set includes two online news sharing sites, specifically Digg and Newsvine, and the other two mainstream media outlets that have both an online and a television presence, namely CNN and the BBC. ⑧ The paper begins with an overview of these news providers and then turns to a focus on content for a one-week period in Fall 2010.

From a paper by Ping Yu

1. Which sentence(s) would fit in the general to specific progression given in Figure 2?

Sentence numbers

General statement(s): _____

Detail or commentary related to the general statement(s): _____

More specific detail or commentary: _____

Broader statement(s), purpose or aims: _____

2. What is your reaction to the quote before the start of the introduction?[1] Do you think it serves a useful purpose?

3. How good is the fit between the first and second paragraphs? In Sentence 6, what would be the effect of eliminating the phrase *To explore this issue*?

4. What is the purpose of the second paragraph? What term is used to describe such paragraphs? Do you think such paragraphs are helpful?

5. What would be the effect of simply starting with the second paragraph?

6. Does the introduction suggest that the student is engaged in the topic and will possibly have something relevant to say about it? Why or why not?

In order to establish relevance, it is important to lead your reader to the focus of your work. This requires some careful attention to not only the overall progression of ideas from general to specific, but to the information flow or connection between sentences.

---

[1] This is called an epigraph. This book also starts with an epigraph that is generally attributed to the ancient Greek philosopher, Plato.

Language Focus: Old to New Flow of Ideas

You may have noticed that the introduction in Task Two is rather easy to follow. To some extent, this may be due to the topic, which may be familiar to you as a user of the Internet. Another factor, however, is the order of information in the sentences. Take a look at this section of the introduction.

③ . . . we are in the "Web 2.0" period of the Internet era, in which we are influenced by social networking sites (Facebook and MySpace), online video sharing (YouTube), as well as online news sharing sites (Digg). ④ One of the key differences between Web 2.0 and the previous Web 1.0 era is that in the Web 1.0 period most users were simply acting as consumers of content, while now any participant can be a content creator in Web 2.0 due to the many technological aids designed to maximize the potential to produce content (Cormode & Krishnamurthy, 2008). ⑤ Since Internet users are now empowered to be either creators or selectors of content, there has been ongoing debate as to whether traditional news media still have the power to strongly shape public opinion.

⑥ To explore this issue, this paper examines the overlap and divergence of content on two online news sharing sites, specifically Digg and Newsvine, and content in two mainstream media outlets that are both online and on television: CNN and the BBC. ⑦ The paper begins with an overview of these news providers and then turns to a focus on content for a one-week period in Fall 2010.

The sentences in the text follow a pattern of old to new information flow in which old or previously stated information is at the beginning of the sentence and the new information is more toward the end.

Sentence 3: . . . . we are in the "Web 2.0" period of the Internet era, in which we are influenced by social networking sites (Facebook and MySpace), online video sharing (YouTube), as well as online news sharing sites (Digg).

Sentence 4: One of the key differences between Web 2.0 and the previous Web 1.0 era is that in the Web 1.0 period most users were simply acting as consumers of content, while now any participant can be a content creator in Web 2.0 due to the many technological aids designed to maximize the potential to produce content (Cormode & Krishnamurthy, 2008).

Web 2.0 was new information in Sentence 3, but once the sentence has been read, *Web 2.0* becomes old information that is picked up in Sentence 4. A similar pattern is seen between Sentences 4 and 5. The new information in Sentence 4 is *any participant* and this is picked up again in Sentence 5, which begins with *Internet users*—the same group as *any participant*.

Sentence 4: One of the key differences between Web 2.0 and the previous Web 1.0 era is that in the Web 1.0 period most users were simply acting as consumers of content, while now any participant can be a content creator in Web 2.0 due to the many technological aids designed to maximize the potential to produce content (Cormode & Krishnamurthy, 2008). Since Internet users are now empowered to be either creators or selectors of content, there has been ongoing debate as to whether traditional news media still have the power to strongly shape public opinion.

Between Sentences 5 and 6, we see the same pattern, even though the sentences are in different paragraphs. An important variation here, however, is that the summary phrase *this issue* is used to restate the idea presented in Sentence 5.

Since Internet users are now empowered to be either creators or selectors of content, there has been ongoing debate as to whether traditional news media still have the power to strongly shape public opinion.

To explore this issue, this paper examines the overlap and divergence of news content on two sets of news sources representing different media.

So, what you are aiming for is a way of ordering information comparable to what we see in this paragraph.

For many people the purpose of

Familiar/old information

museum displays is to provide the public an opportunity

to view treasures from the past.

Familiar/old information—same as *displays* → New Information

Museum exhibitions also serve to educate people about science,

Familiar/old information

culture, or nature. The goal of museum displays for curators,

New information

however, often is directed at presenting collections of objects that

Now familiar information—repetition of *stories*

when placed together tell stories. These stories or narratives can

New information

be quite powerful in terms of communicating ideas and creating

Now familiar information—repetition of *creating knowledge*

new knowledge about the display topics. This construction of

New information

knowledge is of great significance to the evolution of ideas and

scholarship.

Although you may be concerned that you should avoid repetition in your writing, repetition that results from old to new information flow can facilitate reading and generally goes unnoticed when done well. Old to new patterns of information flow establish bridges between ideas and allow you to move smoothly from general to specific in one paragraph or over several paragraphs. Old to new information flow also meets the expectations of good readers who generally anticipate what information is to come in subsequent sentences. To give you a better idea of how to achieve this kind of information sequence, we offer this next task.

Task Three

Work though this exercise, which focuses on using old to new information flow to establish a clear connection of ideas. Compare your answers with those of a partner if you can.

1. Let's imagine that you are going to write about why people often misjudge how much time it takes to complete a task. You begin with this first sentence.

   ①When we need to complete a task, we often have a rather unrealistic idea of how long it will take to finish it.

   What information should the next sentence begin with to meet the reader's expectation? Think about the old to new pattern of organizing information. List the possibilities here.

2. Which of these possibilities for Sentence 2 seems best? Why?

   ②a The planning fallacy[2] (Bueler et al., 2002) is something we all have had to face.

   ②b We all have had to deal with the planning fallacy (Bueler et al., 2002).

   ②c This phenomenon is known as the planning fallacy (Bueler et al., 2002).

   ②d According to Bueler et al. (2002), the planning fallacy is faced by everyone.

---

[2] A mistaken belief

3. Which of these two would you prefer for Sentence 3? Why?

   ③a We often underestimate the time needed for a number of reasons.

   ③b The planning fallacy exists for a number of reasons.

4. What would be a logical content focus for Sentence 4?

5. Read these two versions of the beginning of the introduction. Which do you prefer? Why?

   A. ① When we need to complete a task, we often have a rather unrealistic idea of how long it will take to finish it. ② The planning fallacy (Bueler et al., 2002) is something we all have had to face. ③ We often underestimate the time needed for a number of reasons. ④ We need to overcome the planning fallacy to prevent problems.

   B. ① When we need to complete a task, we often have a rather unrealistic idea of how long it will take to finish it. ② This phenomenon is known as the planning fallacy (Bueler et al., 2002). ③ The planning fallacy exists for a number of reasons. ④ One has to do with a lack of experience.

6. For both Versions A and B, try to guess where the paper might be headed? What would you envision as a Sentence 5 for each version?

There are two final, but important, points we need to stress here. First, in considering how to create a good sequence of ideas, you should attempt to establish an old to new pattern of information flow. If this is not possible, you can connect ideas using one of the standard linking phrases such as *therefore* and *however*. These linking phrases can help you alert your readers that you may violate their expectations in terms of the old to new content. Despite the apparent attractiveness of using linking phrases, we suggest that these not be your predominant strategy for showing connections between ideas. If you look at well-written texts in your own field, you will likely notice that authors do not use that many linking phrases. To sum up the first point, bear in mind a and b on page 11.

a. Old information can be repeated in a summary of previous information in several ways: exact or almost exact repetition, repetition through synonyms, or repletion through *this* + NOUN. Each of these forms of repetition can be highly effective.

b. If it is not possible to pick up some old information and the focus must shift, use a logical connector.

Our second important point is that, for some writers, old to new information flow is intuitive; for others, writing in this manner requires quite a lot of effort. If you are in the latter group, we suggest you first write with an emphasis on your audience, purpose, and content. Once your ideas are fairly clear, then revise to establish a good old to new flow of information. If you try to have both good content and flow of ideas simultaneously, you may put too great a burden on yourself to get the text just right, which can impede your writing progress. Keep in mind that writing is a process that takes time.

Task Four

This task presents the first two paragraphs of a draft of an introduction from a course paper focusing on the protection of biodiversity. You may notice that the second paragraph reads a bit more smoothly than the first. This underscores the fact that opening paragraphs are particularly challenging to write because there are so many possible starting points. Using what you have learned so far about old to new information flow, revise the first paragraph so that the information connection from one sentence to the next is clear. Make any small changes you like to the second paragraph as well.

① National parks and reserves play a vital role in conserving biodiversity worldwide. ② Founded in 1948, the International Union for Conservation of Nature (IUCN) lists over 100,000 sites (11.5% of the Earth's land surface) in the World Database on Protected Areas (World Resource Institute, 2004). ③ The role of conserving biodiversity was not central until the 1990s when the IUCN changed the definition of a PA. ④ A PA is defined as "an area of land and/or sea especially dedicated to the protection and maintenance of biological diversity, and of natural and associated cultural resources, and managed through legal or other effective means" (Dudley and Philips, 2006). ⑤ A "fences and fines" approach is the most common method for protecting these areas. ⑥ People are therefore excluded from protected areas by drawing boundaries and penalizing those who enter, thus discouraging human encroachment.

⑦ However, these traditional approaches have failed to balance the conservation objective with the livelihoods of local communities denied access to the natural resources in the protected areas. ⑧ Through the 1970s and 1980s, the conservation community increasingly realized that protected area management needs to include support for impoverished people who live in or adjacent to PAs and are dependent on the local natural resources within these areas. ⑨ The concept of Integrated Conservation and Development Projects (ICDPs) was developed (Brandon and Wells, 1992; Mogelgaard, 2003) to address this need.

Points of Departure: Starting the Introduction

Of course, there are several ways to begin a text, some of which may be more common in some fields than in others. For instance, research on law review article introductions found that authors often begin by offering definitions, general statements of fact, stories about people, or descriptions of hypothetical situations (Feak et al., 2000). In a more recent study, James Hartley (2009) examined first sentences of published papers in psychology, chemistry, and physiology and identified no fewer than 13 kinds of openings.

Task Five

Here are some possible types of first sentences or openings to an introduction. Mark with a check (✓) those that you think would be appropriate in your field for a course paper and/or for a research article for publication or a proposal (consider either a dissertation proposal or a small grant proposal to fund travel to a conference, or another research proposal).

	Course Paper or Project Report	Proposal	Publication
1. a surprising idea or statistics, particularly those highlighting a problem or unusual finding	_____	_____	_____
2. a comment on the scope or focus of past or current research	_____	_____	_____
3. a story about real people and their experience (or even one focusing on yourself)	_____	_____	_____
4. common knowledge in your field	_____	_____	_____
5. a definition	_____	_____	_____
6. a question that engages the reader	_____	_____	_____
7. an opinion regarding research findings	_____	_____	_____
8. a reference to a single study, a quote, or a leading scholar	_____	_____	_____
9. a comment on research directions or orientations	_____	_____	_____
10. a statement indicating the purpose of the paper	_____	_____	_____

Can you think of any other ways to open?

Now look at these openings from research papers. Working from the list, label the opening according to the ten types given. Do any of these make you curious about the paper content? Which, if any, suggest that the author is engaged in the topic?

1. The video game industry has grown at a tremendous rate. _____

2. In recent years, human-computer interaction researchers have given considerable attention to digital photographic practice as a central feature of contemporary home life in Anglo-American societies. _____

3. This study has two purposes: (a) to describe the mental health status of frail elders living at home in Michigan and (b) to identify subgroups of individuals, by sociodemographic and clinical characteristics, who are more likely to experience mental health problems. _____

4. When modeling the dynamics of a complex structure, it is often impractical to perform a finite element analysis of the entire structure. _____

5. Perspectives on the extent of bacterial diversity have expanded substantially in the past decade. _____

6. The bamboo fire cycle hypothesis proposed by Keeley and Bond (1999) argues that lightning-ignited wildfire has synchronized flowering and recruitment of bamboos throughout Asia. _____

7. The problem of autonomous underwater vehicle (AUV) control continues to pose considerable challenges to system designers, especially when the vehicles are underactuated and exhibit large parameter uncertainty. _____

8. Plastic shrinkage is the dimensional change that occurs in
   all fresh cement-based materials within the first few hours
   after placement when the mixture is still plastic and has
   not yet achieved any significant strength.   _____

9. At first sight the hypothesis that television viewing could
   be related to the cycles of the moon might appear to be
   far-fetched, not to say preposterous.   _____

10. It is probably not news to anyone in academia that the
    experience of submitting one's work for publication—
    a high stakes game upon which hiring, promotion, and
    continued employment can depend—is often fraught
    with frustration and disappointment.   _____

Introductions to Course Papers

To gain an understanding of introductions to course papers, we have begun examining the Michigan Corpus of Upper-level Student Papers (MICUSP). MICUSP contains more than 800 papers (approximately 2.3 million words) from a variety of disciplines in Humanities and Arts, Social Sciences, Biological and Health Sciences, and the Physical Sciences. All of the papers received the top grade (A) in the course for which they were written and, therefore, we assume that they meet the standards for good work.

Table 1 shows the kind of paper and kind of introduction associated employed by the student writer for a subsample of 51 papers.

Table 1. Openings in Student Course Papers in MICUSP (N = 51)

Paper Type	Field	Introduction Opening
Argument	Civil and Environmental Engineering	Definition
Argument	Biology	Hypothetical scenario
Argument	Biology	Definition
Argument	Biology	Question
Argument	Biology	Reference to single study
Critique	Civil and Environmental Engineering	Common knowledge
Critique	Physics	Definition
Critique	Economics	Reference to single study
Critique	Economics	Reference to single study
Critique	Civil and Environmental Engineering	Statement of purpose
Essay	Economics	Scope of past research
Other	Civil and Environmental Engineering	Story about a real situation
Proposal	Physics	Definition
Proposal	Biology	Evaluation of research finding
Proposal	Biology	Scope of past research
Report	Physics	Comment on research direction
Report	Physics	Comment on research direction
Report	Economics	Common knowledge

Report	Economics	Common knowledge
Report	Physics	Common knowledge
Report	Mechanical Engineering	Common knowledge
Report	Physics	Common knowledge
Report	Psychology	Common knowledge/surprising statistics
Report	Physics	Definition
Report	Physics	Definition
Report	Psychology	Definition
Report	Psychology	Definition
Report	Economics	Reference to single study
Report	Psychology	Reference to single study
Report	Civil and Environmental Engineering	Statement of purpose
Report	Physics	Statement of purpose (*I* perspective in which the student includes him- or herself)
Report	Civil and Environmental Engineering	Statement of what was done in student's research
Research	Mechanical Engineering	Comment on research direction
Research	Economics	Common knowledge
Research	Mechanical Engineering	Common knowledge
Research	Psychology	Common knowledge
Research	Physics	Definition
Research	Mechanical Engineering	Definition
Research	Mechanical Engineering	Definition
Research	Mechanical Engineering	Hypothetical scenario
Research	Mechanical Engineering	Hypothetical scenario (*I* perspective)
Research	Psychology	Question
Research	Mechanical Engineering	Reference to popular culture
Research	Economics	Reference to single study
Research	Economics	Scope of past research
Research	Physics	Scope of past research
Research	Economics	Statement of fact
Research	Economics	Statement of purpose
Research	Mechanical Engineering	Statement of purpose
Research	Physics	Statement of what was done in student's research (*I* perspective)

Task Six

Look at Table 1, and consider whether there are any trends or tendencies in terms of the field or type of paper and the type of introduction. To help you do this, complete the chart, which presents some of the opening types in the table and reorganizes them. The first row has been done for you. After completing the chart, choose four or five papers that you have recently written and look at how you started. Do you think your openings were effective? Why did you choose the openings of those papers?

Type of Opening	Number of Examples	Papers with at Least Two of the Opening Types	Fields with at Least Two of the Opening Types
Comment on research direction	3	Report	Physics
Common knowledge			
Definition			
Hypothetical scenario			
Question			
Reference to single study			
Scope of past research			
Statement of purpose			
Story about a real situation			

As can be seen in the table, many of the papers begin with some kind of factual information such as a definition, other statement of fact, or a reference to previous research. Fewer papers begin with an immediate focus on the purpose of the paper. This difference may reflect the fact that many writing assignments give students freedom to choose a topic, often in consultation with the instructor. For such papers it would make sense that students need to prepare the reader by providing a backdrop rather than begin with their purpose. For writing assignments that ask students to respond to a prompt (statements and/or questions to which you reply), on the other hand, since the topic has essentially already been justified or established, students may simply begin with their purpose and restate part of the prompt. Even if a topic is given, however, it is still important to consider the opening strategy. In many instances, to make a good first impression it may be best to take only the essence of the prompt and reshape it to create a new context for the paper. The reasons for this may become clear as you work through this next text.

Task Seven

Consider this prompt for a course paper in information science.

> According to recent estimates, well over a million websites are labeled as blogs and this number continues to grow. Today blogs can be found for political campaigns, news, business, and even university courses. While many have argued that blogs are a valuable means of information sharing, others believe that these sites raise serious issues regarding intellectual property. To what extent should blogging lead us to reconsider our views regarding notions of intellectual property?

If you were to respond to this prompt for a course, how would the prompt factor in your introduction? To what extent are your assumptions about your audience relevant in this decision? Consider these three strategies and the related opening sentences that exemplify the strategy.

Would you:

1. restate all or some portion of the prompt

   The number of blogs today has given rise to serious issues in relation to intellectual property, causing us to reconsider our views toward this concept.

2. create an introduction in which you find an opportunity within the prompt to redefine or reshape the topic

   In recent years the Internet has prompted significant changes in the realm of intellectual property rights, including how innovations and ideas should be diffused.

3. challenge the prompt

   Because of the First Amendment of the U.S. Constitution, the issue of intellectual property rights in relation to blogging is essentially a non-issue.

4. simply begin with your purpose?

   This paper discusses how blogging is reshaping our views of intellectual property.

What kind of audience is envisioned for each of these openings? Which of the openings do you think would make a positive impression on a grader?

Clark (2005) suggests that prompts are more like stage directions for an actor, who must "assume a particular role" to interpret those directions and the story that will unfold. In other words, writers need to establish a need or a basis for writing and "pretend" that it is this need rather than the prompt itself that has generated the response. This, of course, may require a writer to take on the role of an expert, a knowledgeable member of the field, or minimally someone who is engaged with the topic at hand (roles that may be unfamiliar or uncomfortable for some students). In fact, as Clark argues, for many instructors an unstated expectation of many course writing assignments is that students will take on an appropriate writing persona. (Note that another expectation of your instructor is that you will connect your paper to the course reading and broader themes that have emerged or are emerging from class discussion.)

By the end of the introduction the larger point that you intend to develop should be clear. This larger point, also referred to as your thesis statement[3], should indicate the position or opinion you have about your topic rather than express a fact. Note how in the concluding sentence of this introduction, the student very clearly indicates his position on the issue of drugs in the water system and the need for stricter standards.

The presence and fate of pharmaceutically active compounds (PhACs) in the aquatic environment has been recognized as a serious public policy issue. Although PhACs have been reported to occur in both ground and drinking water samples, their direct biological effects on humans remains unclear, particularly among those most vulnerable in society: the elderly, pregnant women and young children. Thus, regulatory authorities must begin to set stricter allowable limits of PhACs that are well below levels with any likelihood of posing health risks.

---

[3] There are many good websites that discuss the creation of strong thesis statements. While most of these are directed at undergraduate student writers, many offer advice that is applicable to graduate-level writing.

Task Eight

This task is based on a paper from MICUSP. First, read the writing prompt, which was given as an assignment in a graduate psychology class. Then read the introduction to the student's response, and answer the question at the end. Note that psychopathology involves the study of mental illness or mental distress, or the manifestation of behaviors and experiences that may indicate the presence of mental illness or psychological impairment.

> There have been growing international efforts over the years to not only understand and treat physical illness, but to also understand and treat mental illness. Consider whether or not there should be a universal requirement to study and treat psychopathology in adults all over the world. Provide three reasons for and three reasons against. Be specific and cite your readings.

> While I think that international research can be useful for psychological researchers in the United States and other countries, I also feel that researchers in the United States or any other country cannot or should not "require" the study of psychology in adults all over the world. Similarly, while I think that there may be a greater demand for the treatment of psychopathology worldwide, I don't think that we can or should implement a universal "requirement" to treat psychopathology in adults all over the world. Here is why.

1. How well has the student positioned herself as a knowledgeable member of the discipline? What is your impression of the student?

2. What assumptions has the student made about her audience?

3. This introduction seems rather conversational in tone. Would you agree? And if so, do you think this is a good strategy for a graduate student?

4. What is your reaction to the use of *I* here?

Finally, we should note that in the MICUSP data shown in Table 1, there seems to be no strong association between the type of paper and the type of introduction. This conclusion, however, should be viewed with some caution since MICUSP does not contain the assignment details. For instance, we do not know which papers were responses to a prompt and which were responses to topics chosen by the students.

Task Nine

An international student has asked several friends for some feedback on his introduction to an information science course paper that focuses on email overload. For this assignment students were free to choose their own focus within the broader topic of problems related to the management of information resources. Read the feedback that he received and consider whether you agree or disagree. Ignore any issues related to grammar in the student's text. (Note that email is spelled with and without the hyphen in this text.)

The Personal Information Management of E-mail: An Exploratory Study

Tze-Hsiang Lin

1. Introduction

① As a product of information technology, electronic mail (e-mail) is a widely commonly used communication medium for task cooperation and personal interaction. ② Nowadays, it's safe to say the importance of e-mail and telephone is regarded the same in the workspace. ③ That is, people without e-mail may be slowly losing contact with outside world like people don't use telephone. ④ According to Mano and Mesch (2009), "We can conclude, then, that email, as a technological means to improve the lives of individuals and employees, has proved beneficial in many areas, providing better use of time, and fluidity in correspondence"(p. 68). ⑤ There is no doubt that e-mail allows people to transmit important information more rapidly than using fax or snail-mail. ⑥ People can send and receive their e-mail anytime and

anywhere as long as they have the access to the Internet. ⑦ Furthermore, the monthly postage bill will be considerable reduced once people chose e-mail to satisfy their mail communication needs.
⑧ However, while people experience many advantages in communicating via e-mail, there are lots of disadvantages existing in this technology. ⑨ Long before e-mail is widespread in our today's daily life, Pliskin's (1989) study has found the following: When E-mail works well it is a user's dream, i.e. a tool that help cope with geographical and temporal boundaries. ⑩ Unfortunately, E-mail can also be a user's nightmare. (p. 271) ⑪ This suggests that e-mail has it own limitations and drawbacks.

⑫ In addition, the broader study of the impacts of contemporary information technologies reveals that e-mails is now more than just a communication tool for users. ⑬ According to Whittaker and Sidner (1996), "Our empirical data show however, that although email was originally designed as a communications applications, it is now being used for additional functions that it was not designed for, such as task management and personal archiving. ⑭ We call this email overload" (p. 276). ⑮ E-mail overload is prevalent among current e-mail user. ⑯ They include task management, personal archiving and asynchronous communication. ⑰ However, e-mail overload cause troubles for personal information management. ⑱ Too many kind of e-mail, such as conversational threads, outstanding tasks and unread documents, clutter in user's inbox (Whittaker and Sidner, 1996, p. 276).

Student 1

I think this is an okay start, but it's a bit hard to follow your line of thinking. I'm not sure why you mention telephones and postage if your focus is on the issue of having to deal with email overload. Can you start with a sharper focus?

Student 2

I don't think your first paragraph is doing much to situate your discussion. Why not just start with the second paragraph?

Student 3

I like what you have here. You've connected your point to the real world, which is good. Also you have connected your topic to other research. This should work.

Student 4

Some of your points in the first paragraph don't seem necessary (e.g., people without email may be slowly losing contact with outside world). You need to lead your reader to your point more efficiently. Even your second paragraph could be better organized. You have some nice quotes, but they are lost in the middle.

Your reaction? Rewrite the introduction to address what you think are the most important concerns.

Introductions to Book Reviews

Book reviews are common assignments in some university courses, especially those in the social sciences; book reviews are also one of the first publications for many scholars. While a complete discussion of book reviews is not possible here, we do think that it is worthwhile to focus on introductions to this genre.[4]

We looked at the book reviews in MICUSP and found that those written for a course tend to begin in one of two ways.

1. a focus on the book

   In *Cognitive Development and Learning in Instructional Contexts*, Byrnes (2001) lays out a connectionist view of literacy, drawing primarily upon the model of Seidenberg and McClelland (1989). This model conceptualizes reading as the product of the interaction of four processors—the orthographic (visual symbols), meaning (word meanings), phonological (graphophonemic), and context (knowledge of language pragmatics, semantics, syntax).

2. a comment on the place of the book in the field

   Edward W. Said's *Orientalism*, despite and perhaps because of its controversial and polemical nature, has achieved its own authoritative status in today's academia. Many historians of "the Orient" have adopted concepts and views expressed in *Orientalism* in their own works.

In published book reviews, however, we tend to see more variety in the introductions.

---

[4] For more general guidance on writing book reviews, see Unit 6 of *Academic Writing for Graduate Students*.

Task Ten

As identified by Motta-Roth (1998) and others, different kinds of information can provide the backdrop for published book reviews, some examples of which are given here. The different kinds of information can be used alone or in combination with each other. Which of these would you likely choose for a book review for publication in a journal in your field? Which do you think could also be used in a book review for a course in your field? Why?

1. Summarizing the focus

   This book provides a review of the principal transport issues affecting rural areas (Chapters 2–7) and the implications of transport policy in the countryside (Chapters 8–14). Its context is largely British, although there are a few comparative case studies drawn from abroad.

2. Describing potential readership or talking about "the reader"

   a. This book is intended for anyone interested in knowing more about the development of pharmaceutical medicines. It is an especially good read for those skeptical of the pharmaceutical industry, as it provides a view of the industry that is not heard much in today's media. It can be easily understood by both healthcare professionals and laypersons without any healthcare background.

   b. As the potential reader may suspect from the play on words in the title, the author has a British sense of humor. Indeed, his book "re-examine[s] some of the key principles of the British disability rights movement" (p. 198). I recommend reading the succinct chapter 13 "Concluding Thoughts" first, for a perspective on this thoughtful and thought-provoking book. It is generally accessible and well-written, notwithstanding a number of misspelled words and grammatical oddities. Electronic and print versions are available.

3. Providing information about the author(s)

   As the author of a leading Money and Banking textbook and a Federal Reserve Governor, Frederick Mishkin needs no introduction. This work displays the same clarity of modeling and composition that made his textbook a bestseller. It is a plea for open financial flows; its central message is clear—globalize or languish.

4. Making generalizations about the topic

   Scattering and absorption of light is a big subject and one of growing importance with the rapid growth of optical engineering into most aspects of modern life from bar code readers and CD players to laser printers and phototherapy in medicine as well as material processing by laser beams. Thus this book is addressing a real problem of our time. It does so in a thorough and fundamental manner.

5. Establishing the place of the book in the field

   Previous editions of Anil Chopra's *Dynamics of Structures* set the standard as the textbook of choice for teaching structural dynamics with an eye to earthquake engineering. This third edition has come out nearly eleven years after the first hit the bookshelves, and what a fruitful decade this has been for earthquake engineering (see review of the second edition in *Earthquake Spectra* 17, 549). Performance-based earthquake engineering, which was in its infancy when the first edition of this book was published, is now entering its second generation.

6. Evaluating the book

   Michael Haas' recent book, *International Human Rights*, aims high in providing a comprehensive introduction to the study of international human rights. He succeeds with this volume, which provides an objective, fact-based, and inter-disciplinary introduction to the topic, well suited for undergraduate students and instructors looking for a background and reference type text.

Language Focus: *As*

A close reading of the book review excerpts reveals that **as** was used in four of the examples.

1. It is an especially good read for those skeptical of the pharmaceutical industry, **as** it provides a view of the industry that is not heard much in today's media.

2. **As** the potential reader may suspect from the play on words in the title, the author has a British sense of humor.

3. **As** the author of a leading Money and Banking textbook and a Federal Reserve Governor, Frederick Mishkin needs no introduction.

4. Previous editions of Anil Chopra's *Dynamics of Structures* set the standard **as** the textbook of choice for teaching structural dynamics with an eye to earthquake engineering.

You may also have noticed that **as** does not have the same meaning in all of the examples.

As is commonly used in making comparisons.

The authors were not as clear as they could have been in the opening chapter.

As can also be used to convey

1. Causal relationships

     An important computational issue raised in the volume is the use of large training sets, **as** this can lead to computational problems and degeneracy.

2. Adversative relationships

     Much **as** I admire Schaller's book, I also found it frustrating.

     Strange **as** it may seem, this book is the first monograph about Procopius written in this century.

3. The role or function of someone or something, which in some cases adjusts the strength of a claim or establishes the author as someone deserving of an opinion

     As a former editor of a journal, I disagree with the author's claim that peer review is a seriously flawed process.

     As an introduction to the latest theories, this book has a lot to offer newcomers to the field.

     This book should be required only **as** a supplemental text.

4. Simultaneous events

     I often found myself confused **as** I was reading this book.

5. A connection to a previous point

     As I stated earlier, this work is extremely valuable in the current context of social thought.

As-clauses can also be used to provide a link to a particular section of the extant text or to a different text that offers support for what the writer is saying. These are known as linking as-clauses. (Note the linking **as**-clause at the beginning of Task Ten.)

> The purpose of this handbook, **as** stated in the preface, is to provide a fairly complete documentation for a series of advanced semiconductors.

> **As** acknowledged in the introduction, new research material is not presented in these chapters.

It is important to note that **as**-clauses have no subjects. Compare these two sentences.

> **As** was mentioned previously, this new theory requires little explanation.

> **As** it was mentioned previously, this theory requires little explanation.

Each sentence is grammatically correct, but they have different meanings. The first **as**-clause correctly lacks a subject and simply refers the reader to an earlier point; the second sentence has a subject, **it,** after **as** and together as it is equivalent to **since.**

Task Eleven

Write two short introductions to a review of *Creating Contexts: Writing Introductions across Genres* for two different audiences: (1) readers of a journal in your field and (2) your instructor or students at your institution. You do not need to read through the entire volume to do this task.

Introductions to Critiques and Reviews of Journal Articles and Book Chapters

Our review of journal article and book chapter critiques in MICUSP revealed that students begin their critiques in one of two ways. One is by announcing their purpose as in *The purpose of this paper is to analyze . . .* After announcing the purpose, they then introduce and summarize the article. In the other, the more common of the two, students begin by summarizing the content of the article or chapter and then quickly move to highlighting weaknesses in the work (or less frequently, the strengths), as in this example.

① In his essay, "Music and Negative Emotion," Jerrold Levinson attempts to explain a strange phenomenon: people finding pleasure in music that conveys emotions with normally distressing connotations. ② By explaining the differences between musically aroused emotion and those we usually experience, refuting misleading explanations, and formulating some more reasonable ones of his own, Levinson makes a noble attempt to delve into this curious, yet common occurrence. ③ His investigations yield eight distinct rewards conferred upon a listener of such musical works. ④ While Levinson's essay presents a fairly comprehensive argument, it contains several flaws, leading him to too hastily reject valid arguments, or fail to encompass other useful explanations. ⑤ Although by no means presenting its own unified explanation of the rewards of listening to negatively emotional music, this essay will endeavor to supplement Levinson's line of reasoning.

(From MICUSP PHI.G0.10.1 Music and Negative Emotion)

Note how the student begins with the general focus of the article and some slightly positive comments about the work (the good news) and then uses *while* to introduce the negative commentary (the bad news). Such "*positive statement* BUT *negative statement*" assertions are often used to transition into the primary focus of a discussion (also in introductions to research articles and proposals, as you will see later). Such statements are valuable in that they reveal the direction of the discussion and in the case of a review or critique help clarify your stance toward the text under review.

If you have been asked to review a manuscript for publication, you may also need to write a brief introduction before moving into the detailed evaluation of the manuscript. While we cannot offer an in-depth discussion of peer review[5], it is important to keep in mind that you have at least two audiences for the review, the author(s) of the manuscript and the editor of the journal; if you are a graduate student, you possibly have a third audience, your advisor. In addressing your audiences, you should maintain a professional, helpful voice, rather than an adversarial one. In other words, write as you would to a colleague who has asked for critical feedback.

The peer review process varies somewhat from journal to journal; some journals use the comment feature on Adobe Acrobat Professional; others use a more traditional approach that requires the creation of a written review and a subsequent upload to a journal website. For those producing a written review of this type, we now turn to the writing of the introduction.

Many experienced reviewers begin their reviews with an overview of the paper under review, much like the student papers in MICUSP. Similar to an introduction to a paper for publication, this overview or summary can help readers understand the context of the review. For the manuscript author, your summary reveals what you see as the main message of the paper; for the editor, your summary can serve as a reminder of the manuscript content and may save him or her the added work of reading the manuscript again before reading your evaluation.

---

[5] For a more detailed discussion, refer to *Navigating Academia: Writing Supporting Genres,* University of Michigan Press. Also look for articles on the peer review process in journals in your field.

Task Twelve

Read this introduction to a manuscript review for a business journal. Answer the questions at the end.

Review of "Co-Creation of Value in a Platform Ecosystem: The Case of Enterprise Software"

① The present study poses questions regarding the value of offering complementary goods to a core technology product, such as an online support community for software. ② It asks whether the existence of a support partnership leads to improvement in the technology and under which conditions those who take advantage of complementary support can enjoy more value. ③ This study provides evidence that those who participate in complementary goods attribute greater value to the technology product and that the product experiences increased sales as well as a higher likelihood of an initial public offering on the stock market. ④ This relationship is contingent upon the participant's value appropriation mechanisms—intellectual property protection and downstream capabilities.

⑤ I am pleased to find several strengths in this study. ⑥ Specifically, (i) the research questions that the study raises are quite interesting, (ii) this study tackles a fresh issue that has not been fully studied in our field, and (iii) the author(s) seem to have made a conscious effort to obtain quality data to confirm the hypotheses. ⑦ The empirical investigations have been fairly well conducted with a series of robustness checks, and I believe that this study has the potential to make a meaningful contribution to the literature.

⑧ Having said this, however, I believe that this study is not sufficiently developed for publication in *MIS Quarterly*. ⑨ There are several issues, which are not necessarily serious, but which must be addressed before further consideration of publication. ⑩ For this reason, I would suggest the associate editor make a decision of revise and resubmit with major revision.

From Min-Seok Pang

1. Does the reviewer seem to be addressing the manuscript author in a respectful manner? Why or why not?

2. Has the reviewer adequately prepared the manuscript author for the negative comments? What is your reaction to the phrase *having said this*?

3. Underline the instances of evaluative statements (positive or negative).

4. What verb tense is primarily used in the introduction?

5. What verbs does the reviewer use to introduce the content of the manuscript? What verbs does the reviewer use to introduce his opinion?

6. In Sentence 9, the reviewer states that *there are several issues, which are not necessarily serious, but which must be addressed.* How strong is the statement? Do you view it as very negative, somewhat negative, or neutral? Why did the reviewer include *which are not necessarily serious*?

7. Would your opinion of Sentence 9 be different if it used the phrase *there are several problems* instead?

8. Note the use of *I* in the second and third paragraphs. Does this seem appropriate? What is the effect of using *I*?

9. What do you think Paragraph 4 will focus on?

10. How do reviewers in your field start their manuscript reviews? Ask an experienced reviewer for some input, if you do not know.

Finding the right way to express your overall reaction to the paper can be difficult and is often something many of us agonize over, especially when we recommend that a paper be rejected. In this next task, we ask you to evaluate the statements indicating the author's perspective on a paper under review.

Task Thirteen

Some statements from the introductions of manuscript reviews that indicate the overall direction of the review follow. Evaluate the statements as being very negative (– –), negative (–), neutral (+/–), positive (+), or very positive (++).

_____ 1. Despite its minor shortcomings, this is a superb study.

_____ 2. I believe this paper is flawed, perhaps fatally flawed, because. . . .

_____ 3. Overall, this is a useful paper as there is a paucity of information in the literature on this topic.

_____ 4. As with most surveys, this article has its weaknesses.

_____ 5. The research described in this paper is limited in that it has sacrificed breadth for depth of analysis.

_____ 6. This article suffers from a number of limitations that need to be addressed.

_____ 7. This is a great paper that is well worth publishing as soon as possible provided the authors can submit further supporting data.

_____ 8. This is a nicely designed study with interesting implications.

_____ 9. This is a carefully done study; the data are clean and the conclusions are supported.

_____ 10. This is a very well-written paper, and recommended for publication with a few edits and additions.

_____ 11. Although this is a carefully conducted study, the results and conclusions need to be interpreted with extreme caution.

_____ 12. This paper is a welcome contribution to a growing awareness of the need for more research in this area.

Finally, let's imagine that you are reviewing a paper that you think should definitely be published and you want to use an evaluative adjective to describe the work. Mark with a check (✓) the adjectives that would *strongly suggest* the paper be published.

____ impressive	____ informative	____ nice
____ useful	____ worthwhile	____ outstanding
____ interesting	____ respectable	____ unusual
____ painstaking	____ laudable	____ practical

Introductions to Journal Articles

Over the past several decades, research article (RA) introductions have been the focus of considerable research. The reasons for this vary, but some of the more obvious are that exemplars are widely available and are relatively short in comparison to other parts of an RA. Given the abundance of research, we can safely say that there is a better understanding of RA introductions than of any other part of this genre.

Much of the advice we have given so far about contextualizing and establishing the relevance of your work will hold true for RA introductions. However, unlike some of the other introductions we have discussed, RA introductions in many cases follow a rather predictable sequence of information and aims. Before exploring this, let us first consider how an RA introduction might relate to other parts of the article.

Many empirical research papers follow a pattern something like this.

Figure 3. Typical Sections of an Empirical Research Article

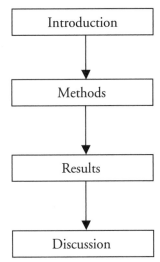

In light of this, you might assume that this is also how a reader might actually read an RA. Ever since Charney's analysis of evolutionists' reading strategies and Bazerman's (1985) work on how physicists read papers, however, it has been very clear that readers of RAs are more likely to scan and make purposeful choices about what they read, selecting what they believe to be "the news." Linear readings of text are not the norm.[6] This notion was in fact well supported at the 2008 Meeting of the Council of Science Editors, where several journal editors and reviewers suggested that actual logical flow of information and selective reading in an empirical RA is in fact something more like that shown in Figure 4.

Figure 4. Connections among Empirical Research Article Sections

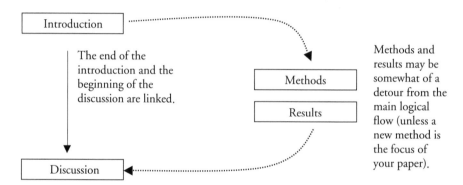

The argument underlying this perspective is that readers may skip the methods and results; they may also skip the introduction, but if they do read it, they will then jump ahead to the discussion. Along the way, they may stop to look at the tables and figures (and acronyms, according to Bazerman). Also important here is that readers may expect some overlap between points made in the introduction and points made in the discussion (Bowen, 2003). Another reason to consider the link between the introduction and the discus-

---

[6] Because readers do not read linearly, they may undermine the rhetorical efforts of an author. Unlike listeners of an oral research presentation who receive information in the order in which it is presented, RAs readers need not wait for what they want to find out in the text (Charney, 1993). Thus, readers can, in effect, control and even distort the flow of the writer's line of reasoning.

sion is that, despite their different purposes, it is in these two sections where you argue for your hypotheses (Neill, 2007). However, typically a significant difference is that your work is *backgrounded* in the introduction and *foregrounded* in the discussion (Lewin, Fine, & Young, 2001), representing a shift in your rhetorical emphasis.

Task Fourteen

What are some advantages of envisioning a connection between the introduction and the discussion section of your RA? Can you think of any disadvantages? Have you noticed this connection in published RA introductions? If you are not sure, look at a few published RAs in your field.

In addition to considering the connection between the introduction and the discussion, you also need to consider how to best contextualize the work you want to publish. Should you just jump right in and tell your readers what your paper is about? Should you highlight a controversy or debate? To what extent should you connect your work with other work in the field? While you will likely see a range of approaches to crafting an introduction, some may be more effective than others and some highly dependent on the kind of work you are presenting (e.g., qualitative as opposed to quantitative work). Moreover, if your stance is controversial, you may need to do more work than if your paper is mainstream. This was clearly shown by Paul (2000) in her examination of published papers on chaos theory, which at the outset had to work harder to establish their position than is typical in other fields.

Task Fifteen

Put together a small reference collection (i.e., a corpus) of 5–15 examples of introductions from one or more journals in your area. Be sure that you collect research articles (i.e., no book reviews, review papers, case reports, or editorials). This corpus will allow you to compare data and texts we present in this volume with those that are most relevant to you. The more texts you compile, the better.

Although not the most harshly criticized section of an RA (that honor generally goes to the discussion section in many fields), manuscript reviewers do not hesitate to point out weaknesses in the introduction. The bulleted list summarizes the common problems of introductions in submitted manuscripts as identified by Johnson and Green (2009), each of whom are editors in chief of a biomedical journal.

- Information that is not relevant to the aims of the study
- Insufficient background or "foundational" research
- Unclear or no stated purpose
- Misplaced information (i.e., information in the introduction should be in another section of the paper, such as the results)
- Length (often because the introduction is considered too long)
- Unsubstantiated claims and personal opinions

We have also noticed that introductions can be criticized for having too many citations. To begin our examination of RA introductions, we now turn to this next task.

Task Sixteen ▬▬▬▬▬▬▬▬▬▬▬▬▬▬▬▬▬▬▬▬▬

Read these five short introductions from the fields of assessment, electrical engineering, education, medicine, and visual culture. Consider whether any of the introductions is close in terms of organization to those of published RAs in your field. Try to describe the organization of each in the space provided. Then, in the Notes section, write about anything that you find interesting in the introduction or that you think could be improved. If you have some concrete suggestions for improvement that could indeed be implemented, list those as well.

1. Kleitman, S. and Stankov, L. (2007). Self-confidence and metacognitive processes. *Learning and Individual Differences,* *17*(2), 161–173.

①This paper examines the relationship between Self-confidence measured during performance on typical cognitive tests and several conceptually related constructs. ②The aim is to further our understanding of Self-confidence and establish its status within the taxonomy of cognitive/metacognitive processes.

③Four lines of evidence will be considered. ④First, we shall argue that Self-confidence is a broad psychological trait that cuts across diverse cognitive domains. ⑤Second, we shall examine the broadness of the Self-confidence construct and, in particular, whether it can be extended to beliefs about the veracity of predictions of events that may or may not happen in the future. ⑥Third, we shall look at the relationship between the Self-confidence factor and measures of broad Self-concepts captured by our own Memory and Reasoning Competence Inventory (MARCI) and the Metacognitive Awareness Inventory (MAI, Schraw & Dennison, 1994). ⑦These measures are expected to show meaningful correlations with Self-confidence, demonstrating that Self-confidence is related to, but cannot be reduced to, these two metacognitive domains. ⑧Fourth, we shall examine the relationship between Self-confidence, personality dimensions, and measures of Speed of test-taking.

Organization: _____

_____

_____

Notes: _____

_____

_____

2. Nayak. J. and Sahu, S. N. (2006). Electrical characteristics of
   GaAs nanocrystalline thin film. *Solid-State Electronics, 50*(2),
   164–169.

① In recent years, there has been considerable interest in the study
of the inter-facial behavior of nanocrystal based semiconductor devices
[1–3]. ② Large surface to volume ratio of the atoms associated with the
nanocrystals, often influences the device characteristics. ③ Moreover,
interruption of the periodicity at the nanocrystal surface, large surface
density of dangling bonds and modified surface structure have been
responsible for the deviated electrical properties of the nanocrystal
based devices compared to the corresponding bulk devices. ④ In general, the current–voltage and the capacitance–voltage studies are carried
out in order to investigate the inter-facial behavior of the nanoelec-
tronic devices. ⑤ A simple Schottky junction can be fabricated between
a metal and the nanostructured semiconductor in order to study the
above characteristics.

⑥ Although the GaAs nanocrystals, synthesized by several techniques [4–9], have been subjected to detailed structural and optical
characterizations, still no systematic study of their inter-facial behavior,
which is a basic requirement for practical device application, has been
reported yet. ⑦ The present work reports, for the first time, the fabri-
cation of metal/nano-GaAs Schottky junctions followed by the study of
the effect of crystallite size and the inter-facial oxide layers on their
electrical properties.

Organization: _____

_____

_____

Notes: _____

_____

_____

3. Meyer, K. A. (2006) When topics are controversial: is it better to discuss them face-to-face or online? *Innovative Higher Education*, *31*(3), 175–186.

① On a recent airplane trip to the west coast, I was reading *The Tipping Point* by Gladwell (2002). ② It referred to a study that found people who communicate electronically dealt with dissenting opinions differently than people who communicate face-to-face. ③ People with dissenting opinions "expressed their arguments most 'frequently and persistently' when they communicated online . . . [because] expressing a dissenting view in person is much harder socially, in other words, gives that opinion much more credence" (pp. 274–275). ④ Communication online, especially through emails that arrive in large numbers, creates a sense of immunity that "simply makes us value face-to-face communications—and the communications of those we already know and trust—all the more" (p. 275). ⑤ In other words, while face-to-face discussions may be harder sometimes, they are still valued, perhaps more so when topics are controversial.

⑥ Could this process explain how students value their in-class (face-to-face) and online discussions? ⑦ In a conversation with other faculty about this issue, one experienced faculty member asserted confidently that, if the discussion happens to be about something controversial, it is better to do it face-to-face. ⑧ Another faculty member asserted just as confidently that controversial discussions are better held online. ⑨ Their responses did not erase my confusion. ⑩ Therefore, this study was undertaken to see who might be right and why and to find out by asking students to tackle several discussions on controversial topics and to assess whether the setting of the discussion—face-to-face or online—made a difference.

Organization: _____

_____

_____

Notes: _____

_____

_____

4. Newman, A. W., Wright, S. W., Wrenn, K. D., Bernard, A. (2005). Should physicians have facial piercings? *Journal of General Internal Medicine, 20*(3), 213–218.

① While physician appearance may not be the most important aspect of the doctor-patient relationship, it does play a role. ② Studies have shown that patients prefer that their physician wear certain attire such as a name tag and white coat, [1–5] while others have correlated appearance with patients' perceptions of a physician's competence. [6–8] ③ Appropriate physician dress is not a static phenomenon. ④ While the importance of physician appearance has been emphasized since the time of Hippocrates, the style of physician attire has been through dramatic changes. ⑤ At times physician appearance has been unique to the profession and at other times has reflected societal fashion. [1]

⑥ Our present U.S. culture is experiencing a trend of body piercing (i.e., piercing of the body other than the traditional single piercing of a female's earlobes). [9] ⑦ Once associated with counterculture, the popularity of body piercing is increasing within mainstream culture, especially among adolescents and young adults. [9, 10] ⑧ Although the prevalence of body piercing is difficult to ascertain due to its lack of permanency, [11] a recent survey found the prevalence of body piercing at one undergraduate campus to be 51%. [12]

⑨ Visible nontraditional piercings are starting to appear on both physician and nonphysician health care providers. ⑩ This study assesses the attitudes of patients and their visitors regarding physicians with visible body piercings as well as the perception of patients and their visitors of the competency and trustworthiness of physicians with visible piercings. ⑪ Additionally, we have surveyed faculty physicians at our institution about their opinions concerning the appropriateness of facial piercings in the health care setting.

Organization: _____

_____

_____

Notes: _____

_____

_____

5. Kissel, L. (2008). The terrain of the long take. *Journal of Visual Culture* 7(3), 349–361.

① But, to the artist who creates a picture by drawing it from the depths of his soul, time is no longer an accessory; it is not an interval that may be lengthened or shortened without the content being altered. ② The duration of his work is part and parcel of his work. ③ To contract or to dilate it would be to modify both the psychical evolution that fills it and the invention which is its goal. ④ The time taken up by the invention, is one with the invention itself. ⑤ It is the progress of a thought which is changing in the degree and measure that it is taking form. ⑥ It is a vital process, something like the ripening of an idea. (Bergson, 1998[1911]: 340)

⑦ The long take has become the terra incognita of the modern documentary film, a blank space in a practice that devotes itself almost entirely to other properties of the shot. ⑧ And this is contrary to its heritage, for documentary was born in the pleasure of watching such ordinary events as leaves shimmering on a tree or a train arriving at a station. (MacDougall, 1998: 209)

Definition

⑨ Sequence Shot: A long, usually complex shot, often including complicated camera movements and action. ⑩ Also called 'Plan-sequence' (the French term), or Long Take. (Monaco, 1999)

⑪ The tripod and camera are set—or I am standing with camera in hand—in a singular, unchanging position before the subject, anticipating the action that will take place. ⑫ I frame and the camera records what I am waiting for, which is the variable of change.

⑬ In my practice of non-fiction filmmaking, the long take is a process of discovery, enabled by the duration of the frame. ⑭ It is a way to move closer to the possibility of uncovering the essence and significance of things, a gesture towards clarity. ⑮ The long take enables a certain kind of intelligibility that is different from an answer. ⑯ It resists constructing a singular meaning to what is before the camera; instead, the long take is expansive. ⑰ I pull the camera's trigger or press a button and the take begins: in tandem with the camera, I inhabit the time of the shot. ⑱ Minutes accumulate as the camera records, its frame dynamic in the squaring of the image. ⑲ The take ends when I release the trigger or depress the record button a second time. ⑳ The time in-between the beginning and end of the take extends an opportunity for greater awareness of the subject at hand; it affords time for a mutual exchange between myself and my subject and, by extension, the spectator. ㉑ The practice of capturing a long take sometimes feels like an investigation or experiment—the possibility for deeper knowledge. ㉒ It is a way to order the phenomena of the world: a means to enter into the structuring of chaos and complexity; a means to assimilate information, both visual and socio-political. ㉓ Within the time of the frame, everyday things become visible and one is offered a moment to linger on a question rather than pursue a particular answer. ㉔ The long take is the condition of possibility for drawing closer, in a sympathetic way, to that which is before the camera.

Organization: _____

_____

_____

Notes: _____

_____

_____

Did you have a *so what* reaction (a question as to why the work is relevant) to any of the introductions? Why?

Why Cite the Literature?

Although we may reasonably debate which of the five introductions is most effective, they do have some features in common. Each states the focus of the research that will be discussed and although some of the texts do this more than others, each includes some reference to previously published literature. Why do researchers expend so much effort discussing what others have done?

Task Seventeen

Consider each of these perspectives on citations. With which do you agree (A) or disagree (D)? Mark those about which you are unsure with a question mark (?).

_____ 1. Citations help authors to acknowledge the intellectual property of others and avoid the problem of plagiarism.

_____ 2. Authors show respect to other scholars by including a citation to the previous work.

_____ 3. There is homogeneity in the papers or books that are cited in published work on a particular topic. Authors tend to cite the same small percentage of papers or other publications in their field.

_____ 4. Citations add strength to an author's ideas and claims.

_____ 5. Citations reflect social networks: Authors often refer to papers by authors with whom they are personally acquainted.

_____ 6. The choice of citations may be motivated by various kinds of pressure. For instance, graduate students may feel compelled to cite advisors, while other authors may avoid citations to the work of competing research groups.

_____ 7. Citations help an author demonstrate that he or she is a well-informed member of a discipline or interdisciplinary field.

_____ 8. Self-citation can be beneficial for an author.

_____ 9. Authors use citations to demonstrate how their work advances the knowledge base of a field.

As the previous task indicates, authors have a quite a lot to think about when choosing the previous work to include in the introductions (more on this issue is presented on pages 59–66). Another consideration, as suggested by the sample introductions, is where in the introduction to indicate your purpose. If you indicate your purpose at the end of the introduction, then how should you begin? To shed light on these questions we now turn to the introduction in Task Eighteen. The introduction is from a paper that investigates self-citation—a practice in which the author himself engages.

Task Eighteen

Read the introduction, and work through the questions and mini-tasks. Both the paragraphs and sentences have been numbered for ease of analysis.

Medoff, M.H. (2006). The efficiency of self-citations in economics. *Scientometrics*, *69*(1), 69–84.

Introduction

(1) ① Citation analysis is a well-established method of evaluating research quality in economics. ② Numerous articles have used citations to assess the quality of economics departments (Scott and Mitias, 1996), economics journals (Laband and Piette, 1994b), academic economists (Medoff, 1989), and to predict Nobel laureates in economics (Quandt, 1976). ③ Citations have also been used to investigate whether favoritism is present in the review process of journals (Laband and Piette, 1994a), if collaboration enhances the quality of economics research (Medoff, 2003), and the monetary returns to economists from publishing articles of varying quality (Sauer, 1988).

(2) ④ The methodological rationale for using citations as an indicator of research quality is that it is argued that a citation represents objective and quantifiable evidence that a subsequent author deemed the article germane to the current research frontier and

relevant in extending this frontier (Diamond, 1986).* ⑤ Anecdotal
evidence suggests that academic economists generally believe that the
number of times an article has been cited is an indicator of its quality and significance. ⑥ Most of the leading economists discussing
their classic articles expressed the opinion that the scientific contribution these classic articles had on the economics literature was evi-
dent from the number of citations their articles had received (Gans
and Shepherd, 1994). ⑦ Blaug and Sturges (1982) used citations as
the criteria for inclusion in their *Who's Who in Economics* dictionary:
"We have therefore selected almost all the living economists in this
dictionary on the grounds that they have had the greatest impact on
their colleagues as revealed by the high frequency with which they
are cited" (p. viii).

(3) ⑧ One area of general agreement among academic economists
is their attitude regarding self-citations (referencing one's earlier
articles in a subsequent article). ⑨ Most academic economists
believe studies using citations should disregard or exclude self- citations. ⑩ The underlying reasons for dismissing self-citations, however, differ. ⑪ Laband (1990) argues that "[f]ollowing the premise
that what an entrepreneur thinks of his/her product bears little
relation to the market reception of the product . . . " self-citations
should be excluded (p. 347). ⑫ Davis and Papanek (1984) maintain that because there is no guaranteed minimum citation standard, self-citations would count as much as the citations of others.
⑬ As a consequence, "the contributions
of vainglorious economists will thus be overrated" (p. 226).
⑭ Similarly, Bodenhorn (2003) contends that self-citations are
purely self-serving and including them would overestimate the
research significance of compulsive self-citers. ⑮ Johnson (1997)
argues that self-citations should be omitted, otherwise there could

be an endogenous inflation in them as authors recognize that article citations have both a monetary (positive effect on earnings) and nonmonetary (professional standing) value.

(4) ⑯ Given the important role, particularly in personnel decisions, that citations play in evaluating the research quality of academic economists it is somewhat surprising that there is no empirical study on the efficacy of self-citations. ⑰ Are self-citations an effective form of advertising? ⑱ Do prior self-citations affect an author's citation count in a subsequent article? ⑲ Does the impact

of a self-citation depend on the prestige of the journal it appeared in or the vintage of the self-citation? ⑳ The purpose of this paper is to empirically answer these questions.

---

* The limitations of using citations as a measure of quality have been discussed and dismissed by Leibowitz and Palmer (1988). They ask rhetorically if an article is a high-quality scientific contribution, then why does it have only a few citations?

1. What is the purpose of each of the paragraphs?

   Paragraph 1 _____

   Paragraph 2 _____

   Paragraph 3 _____

   Paragraph 4 _____

2. The author asks a number of questions at the end. What do you think of this strategy? Could you do this in an RA in your field?

3. The introduction contains two definitions. What are these? Do you think the definitions are necessary? Why or why not? Why do you suppose the author used two different approaches to defining the concepts?

4. Where do the citations occur? Are they concentrated in one part of the introduction or in various locations?

5. The paper follows the APA author-date style of citation. Where are the cited authors' names placed? Why? How prominent are author names in citations in your field?

6. The introduction contains quotes in the second and third paragraphs. Why do you suppose the author used quotes instead of putting the ideas in his own words?

7. What verbs did the author use to report information from other studies? Do you think these same verbs are commonly used in your field?

8. What verb tense (e.g., present or past) and aspect (e.g., perfect) were used in sentences referring to other literature? Why?

9. What is the function of *given* in Sentence 16? What is *anecdotal evidence* (Sentence 5)?

10. Are there any expressions that indicate what the author thinks about the state of knowledge regarding citation in the field? In other words, do we get a sense of the author's stance?

11. What is your reaction to the notion that "the number of times an article has been cited is an indicator of its quality and significance"?

12. How is self-citation viewed in your field?

As you identified what the author wanted to accomplish in each of the paragraphs in the self-citation introduction, you may have thought that the author's aims seemed somewhat familiar (for instance, establishing the topic via citations and indicating that there is a lack of a certain kind of research). Indeed, the introduction follows the model given in Table 2 and is an approach that many writers will use to accomplish three "moves,"[7] often in the order given.

Table 2. Moves in Empirical Research Paper Introductions

Move 1 Establishing a research territory

    a. showing that the general research area is important, central, interesting, problematic, or relevant in some way (optional)

    b. introducing and reviewing items of previous research in the area (obligatory)

Move 2 Establishing a niche[a] (citations to previous literature possible)

    a. indicating a gap in the previous research

    b. extending previous knowledge in some way

Move 3 Presenting the present work (citations to previous literature possible)

    a. outlining purposes or stating the nature of the present research (obligatory)

    b. listing research questions or hypotheses (PISF[b])

    c. announcing principal findings (PISF)

    d. stating the value of the present research (PISF)

    e. indicating the structure of the RP (PISF)

[a]In ecology, a niche is a particular microenvironment where a particular organism can thrive. In our case, a niche is a context where a particular piece of research makes particularly good sense.

[b]PISF = Probable In Some Fields, but rare in others.

---

[7]A move in both written and spoken discourse is a unit that performs a communicative function. It can consist of a clause or one or more sentences.

The CaRS Model

The moves outlined in Table 2 constitute a simple version of what is known as the CaRS model (Swales, 1990, 2004),[8] the aim of which is to Create a Research Space, hence CaRS.

Another three-move model proposed by Lewin, Fine, and Young (2001) is also worth introducing here. Although similar to CaRS, this model describes the moves differently, suggesting that writers

1. first claim that the area of inquiry has relevance (Move 1)

2. establish the research gap that the new research will fill (Move 2)

3. conclude by previewing the new accomplishments (Move 3).

At first glance, the models do seem rather formulaic, suggesting that enacting them is a rather straightforward process. In reality, quite a lot of rhetorical skill is needed to implement them well. One source of difficulty is that you need to indicate that there is a body of previous work with which your work is connected, but which needs to be characterized as being incomplete in some way so that your gap seems important enough to address. Another challenge is that the models are simplified versions of what might be done in reality (as with any model) and they lack specificity. For instance, using the CaRS model, Samraj (2002) analyzed RAs in conservation biology and wildlife behavior and found that authors in these fields may include in their introductions some "positive justification" in which explicit positive reasons for undertaking the study are given. Yet another variation has to do with formatting where in some fields the introduction may have subheadings indicating different sections, such as the literature review. Despite the possible disciplinary variations, we believe that the lack of specificity of the models is offset by gains in clarifying some of the common goals in writing an introduction. Thus, the models serve as a useful basis for further discussion.

Note how the model overall follows the general to specific flow of information, as discussed previously on page 3. In the models each move offers more specific information than the one before it. However, here again it is important to acknowledge variation. Although some introductions might follow the moves in the order proposed and then conclude, in some fields, Moves 1 and 2 may be recycled (repeated) or the moves may appear in a different order.

---

[8]Another more elaborate version is available in Swales (2004).

Task Nineteen

Here are some potential areas for inclusion in the introduction that have been proposed by several researchers. Consider whether or not these are typical or likely in your field. Mark those that are likely with a ✓+, those that are unlikely with a ✓−, those that may optionally be used with a ✓, and those about which you are unsure with a question mark (?).

_____ 1. A discussion of examples to illustrate the topic (Anthony, 1999; Árvay and Tankó, 2004)

_____ 2. Definitions of important terms (Anthony, 1999; Duszak, 1997)

_____ 3. An evaluation of the research presented (Anthony, 1999).

_____ 4. A description of data analysis procedures (Li and Ge, 2009)

_____ 5. A description of the methodology (Ayers, 2008)

_____ 6. Asserting your right to fill the gap as in "As the recipient of an Arts and Humanities Grant, for a project entitled 'Translators as Cultural Agents in the Global Information Age,' I have addressed this question . . . " (Corbett, 2007)

_____ 7. A discussion of a theoretical framework (Árvay and Tankó, 2004)

_____ 8. Signaling the newsworthiness or the new contribution of the research as in "Our main claim here is that . . . " (Dahl, 2009)

If any of these were to be included in an RA introduction in your field, in which part of the introduction should they go?

Now, to gain a better understanding of what you might do in your own RAs, we suggest that you do some text analysis on your own.

Task Twenty

Using the reference collection you put together in Task Fifteen, work through these questions to get an idea of the characteristics of RA introductions in your field.

1. To what extent do the introductions follow the CaRS model and include any of the variations proposed in Task Nineteen? Are any of the moves recycled?

2. How would you characterize the flow of ideas? Do you notice an old information to new information pattern?

3. How would you characterize the opening sentences? Do the RAs start with common knowledge? If so, what kind (facts, definitions, generalizations, something else)? A story? One of the other features described on page 19?

4. Do the introductions contain citations to previous literature? If, yes, where in the introduction do the citations occur—in the beginning, middle, or end? Is all of the previous work contained in the introductions or is there a separate literature review that discusses all or most of the relevant work?

5. Do the articles tend to have more integral or non-integral citations? (See pages 59–62 for more on citation types.)

6. In the integral citations, which verbs are used to report the work of others?

7. How common are definitions? Do they seem necessary?

8. Are there any comments regarding agreement or debate in the field? Do you see any other instances of the authors' perspective toward a point or larger idea?

9. To what extent do the authors seem to be "present" in the text? In other words, do you have a sense of a person behind the words in the texts?

Citation Practices

As you already know, RA introductions nearly always contain citations to other papers or work related to the paper focus. There are a number of reasons for referring to previous literature, many of which were highlighted in Task Seventeen. It is important in RA introductions to put together citations to create a research story that leads your reader to the conclusion that your own research contributes to that story. In other words, recall the main title of this volume, which emphasizes *creating contexts.*

Citations should be chosen for a very particular purpose rather than included simply due to a sense of obligation. The reasons for choosing to cite certain papers varies according to discipline (Harwood, 2010). However, research has shown that these reasons often fall into one of two broad categories (and sometimes fall into both), one is to reward the author(s) of the work cited and the other is to build a more persuasive paper; in other words citations have a rhetorical purpose. Types of reward citation would include several identified by Harwood (2010), each of which serves a different function.

- Advertising one's work or that of others (e.g., citations to an advisor's papers, papers from your research group, or papers written by your friends)
- Crediting those to whom the author is indebted
- Signposting that directs readers to relevant detailed information that the new paper will not delve into

Specific types of citation identified in Harwood's work that fall into the category of rhetorical use include

- Positioning, in which perspectives and findings of others are identified
- Supporting, in which an author justifies the research topic
- Aligning, in which an author indicates an allegiance to a school of thought or a particular side of a debate

Citations can also serve as space savers (Harwood, 2010) that can direct readers to other more detailed information and serve as a "discipline's shorthand for certain ideas" (Paul, 2000) and information. They also carry with them the reputation of the cited author(s) and perhaps the journal in which an article is published (Paul, 2000).

Thus, it is reasonable to conclude that citations are much more than a name and a year (or number). By considering the different functions of citations, you have the opportunity to contextualize your work within the field or discourse community and construct a convincing paper.

Citations are by their very nature a form of old information. Like the old to new paradigm of information flow introduced earlier, once an article is read, the information it contains is potentially familiar information that can be picked up and used to introduce new information, namely your work. Thus, you choose literature that situates your work, while ignoring work that does not. This does not mean that you never cite research that runs contrary to your own. Occasionally, citing such work allows you to set up an argument that you then proceed to tear down (i.e., a straw man argument) (Winsor, 1993). Whether to refer to work with which you disagree or that is in opposition to yours, however, depends on the discipline. In some fields (chaos theory, for instance), silence or a lack of a reference to opposing work is preferred to a refutation of that work (Paul, 2000).

Citation practices vary across disciplines and genres, as demonstrated by Thompson and Tribble (2001), who compared citation practices in RAs (as indicated in Hyland's 1999 study) and PhD dissertations. Some of the results are presented in Table 3.

Table 3. Number of Citations in the Hyland (1999) and Thompson (2000) Corpora

Discipline	Average Number per Paper	Average per 1,000 Word RAs
Mechanical Engineering	27.5	7.3
Physics	24.8	7.4
Electronic Engineering	42.8	8.4
Marketing	94.9	10.1
Philosophy	85.2	10.8
Applied Linguistics	75.3	10.8
Sociology	104.0	12.5
Biology	82.7	15.5
	Average Number per Dissertation	Average per 1,000 Words of Dissertations
Agricultural Botany	248.8	9.04
Agricultural Economics	333.5	5.25

Thompson and Tribble (2001)

As can be seen in Table 3, there are differences between the social sciences and the harder sciences regarding the number and density of citations, with the exception of biology, which is more similar to philosophy than physics in terms of citation use. Interestingly, the two agriculture dissertations also differ in terms of the number and density of citations. Overall, the table also suggests that, regardless of the discipline, there may in general be differences in the citation densities of RAs and dissertations.

Citations in the literature review can take a variety of forms, but one important distinction is that between integral and non-integral citation forms. Integral citations are author-focused and grammatically part of a sentence, as in these examples.

Uluşçu et al. (2009) describe The Bosphorus Strait, the narrow waterway separating Europe from Asia, as one of the world's most congested and difficult-to-navigate waterways in the world.

According to Doğan and Burak (2007), every year, an average of 60,000 vessels, 5500 of which carry oil, liquefied petroleum gas, and other dangerous and hazardous cargo, pass via the Turkish Straits through Istanbul.

Non-integral citations have no grammatical function in a sentence, appearing instead either in parentheses at the end of a sentence or as a number representation with the full reference at the end of the paper, as in these examples.

The Bosphorus Strait has a two-layer current system consisting of the southward upper flow from the Black Sea and the northward lower flow from the Sea of Marmara (Arisoy and Akyarli, 1989; Gregg and Ozsoy, 2002).

The North Anatolian Fault Zone (NAFZ), which is one of the most active dextral fault zones in the world, lies roughly parallel to the Black Sea coast of Anatolia from the Karliova Region in the east to Aegean Sea in the west.

Previous studies have shown the appearance and density of E. huxleyi in the Turkish Straits System and the Black Sea (Aubert et al., 1990; Uysal, 1995; Ünsal et al., 2003; Türkoglu et al., 2004a, b, d).

It has been accepted that the total population of Turkey will reach 110 million by 2030, with an annual increase rate of 2% (Yükse, 2008).

There are some disciplinary differences in terms of the preferred form of citation. As can be seen in Table 4, biology has a very strong preference for non-integral citations, but all of the fields tend to lean in this direction as well, with the exception of philosophy.

Table 4. Ratios of Non-Integral to Integral Citations by Discipline in Hyland (1999) and Thompson (2000)

Discipline	Non-integral	Integral
RAs (Hyland)		
Biology	90.2	9.8
Electronic Engineering	84.3	15.7
Physics	83.1	16.9
Mechanical Engineering	71.3	28.7
Marketing	70.3	29.7
Applied Linguistics	65.6	34.4
Sociology	64.6	35.4
Philosophy	35.4	64.6
Doctoral theses (Thompson)		
Agricultural Botany	66.5	33.5
Agricultural Economics	38.1	61.9

In a study of citation practices in the health sciences, Clugston (2008) found that journals in physiology and radiology tended to have more non-integral than integral citations, while health science journals with a social science focus preferred integral citations; some articles, however, followed neither of these tendencies. Interestingly, even for health science journals that use a numerical referencing system, integral citations were common, contrary to what one might expect. Clugston, therefore, concludes that, despite tendencies, "no hard and fast rule" exists regarding the use of integral and non-integral citations.

The results for the dissertations in Table 4 also do not allow any strong generalizations. However, Charles's 2006 study of citations found that integral citations were by far more common than non-integral in PhD dissertations in both political science and materials science, suggesting that overall integral citations may in fact be preferred in dissertations.

If we can only talk of tendencies, this then raises the question of how to choose between and integral and non-integral citations.

Task Twenty-One

Look at your answer to Question 5 in Task Twenty. Can you discern any reasons for the choice of integral or non-integral citation, if both are used? Do you agree (A) or disagree (D) with the perspectives given here? If you are not sure, place a question mark (?) in the blank.

_____ 1. I should choose to use integral and non-integral citations by considering old to new flow of information.

_____ 2. When I refer to a well-known author, it is best to use an integral citation.

_____ 3. There is a heavy focus on author names in my field, so I should mostly choose integral citations.

_____ 4. I should try to have some variety and switch between both types of citation.

_____ 5. If I want to keep my focus on the work that has been done in my field, I should mostly choose non-integral citations.

_____ 6. I should use mostly integral (or non-integral) citations if that is what most writers in my field do.

Since citations help you to show how your work might contribute to a cumulative scholarly or research process (Feak & Swales, 2009), you may want to give careful consideration to your choice of verb when reporting other work in the field. Indeed, research has shown that reporting verbs can appropriately situate your work in relation to previous work in your field (Thompson & Ye, 1991; Hyland, 1999).

For instance, should you use *state, argue,* or a hedged verb like *suggest?* When choosing a reporting verb, you may want to consider these points:

- There are disciplinary differences in the most common reporting verbs in published articles.
- Reporting verbs can refer to a specific aspect of the cited research (e.g., what the researcher(s) did, what the researcher(s) stated, or what the researcher(s) believes):

Fraser and Greene (2006), focusing upon a broad measure of optimism, *found* that more experienced entrepreneurs were less likely to report optimism. Using a more widely accepted measure of optimism, Cooper et al. (1988) *found* no significant relationship between entrepreneurial experience and reported comparative optimism. Comparing growth expectations with actual growth rates, Landier and Thesmar (2009) *noted* that repeat entrepreneurs (i.e., both sequential and portfolio entrepreneurs) who had started at least one prior business were more optimistic than novice entrepreneurs.

- Reporting verbs can also indicate that you are including the citation to support or strengthen a point or claim for which you are accountable or responsible:

This conclusion is consistent with the large body of evidence *indicating that* social and political skills influence a wide range of outcomes and processes both in organizations (e.g., Ferris, Davidson, et al., 2005; Ferris, Treadway, et al., 2005) and in many nonbusiness contexts (e.g., the decisions of judges and juries concerning defendants; e.g., Downs & Lyons, 1991).

As *described* by Gabriel and Lang (1995), consumption has emerged as an activity of growing importance in the lives of citizens of postindustrial western societies, and constitutes a key element in the process of identity formation.

- Reporting verbs can also convey your interpretation or perspective on the cited work (note that this may be difficult to determine when reading someone else's text unless you are familiar with the cited work):

First, previous research *suggests that* individuals high in social skills are often more persuasive and better able to exercise social influence than persons low in social skills (e.g., Cialdini, 2000; Semadar et al., 2006).

Value-based marketing strategies have been *claimed* to strengthen customer loyalty (Urde, 2003). Some authors have *argued that* such a strategy appears to be more effective for companies that display a "distinct social mission."

In the first example with *suggests* on page 64, the use of the verb *suggest* can indicate the author's lack of commitment to the finding, while in the second, there seems to be a more direct questioning of Urde's position. To make a more neutral statement, instead of *claim*, the verb phrase *described as a means* could have been chosen. In the second sentence, *show, find,* or *demonstrate* would be choices that are less evaluative.

Task Twenty-Two

Here are the most common reporting verbs in published papers from the hard and social sciences.[9] Place a check (✓) next to those you think you can use in a published paper in your field. How many of these did you find in your reference collection?

_____ analyze	_____ focus	_____ report
_____ argue	_____ identify	_____ say
_____ demonstrate	_____ note	_____ show
_____ describe	_____ observe	_____ study
_____ develop	_____ point out	_____ suggest
_____ find	_____ propose	_____ use

Based on Swales, J.M. and Feak, C.B. 2004. *Academic Writing for Graduate Students.* Ann Arbor: University of Michigan Press.

---

[9]Biology, physics, electrical engineering, mechanical engineering, epidemiology, nursing, medicine, marketing, applied linguistics, psychology, sociology, education, and philosophy

Now look at the non-integral citations presented here. Convert each into two integral citations using an appropriate reporting verb, one of which could suggest that you question the claim and one in which your personal perspective is not obvious.

1. A person's attitude toward public cell phone use changes (becomes more accepting) as they use a cell phone more (Isaac et al., 2008).

2. The antecedents and aftermath of banking crises in rich countries and emerging markets have a surprising amount in common (Reinhart & Rogoff, 2008).

3. Employees will be apt to break rules whenever it is in their interest to do so and whenever there are insufficient organizational controls to ensure rule compliance (Eisenhardt, 1989).

4. People are more likely to solve problems with insight if they are in a positive mood than if they are in a neutral or negative one (Subramaniam et al., 2009).

In addition to using the Author + VERB + *that* style of integral citation, you may also consider some of these other forms of integral citations.

According to AUTHOR . . .   In the work of AUTHOR . . .
In the view of AUTHOR . . .   In AUTHOR's analysis of . . .
As indicated by AUTHOR . . .   Following the research of AUTHOR on . . .
In AUTHOR's perspective . . . In line with AUTHOR'S work on . . .

Language Focus: Highlighting Agreement and Disagreement

In our sample text introduction on pages 51–53 you might have noticed that after briefly discussing citation analysis, the author comments on how economists view the issue of self-citation, the focus of the paper.

> ⑧ One area of general agreement among academic economists is their attitude regarding self-citations (referencing one's earlier articles in a subsequent article). ⑨ Most academic economists believe studies using citations should disregard or exclude self- citations. The underlying reasons for dismissing self-citations, however, differ.

You may also already be aware that in literature reviews authors sometimes comment on how a particular issue is viewed in their fields. For instance, an author might indicate that an issue is being hotly debated or has generally been ignored.

Why would authors want to make statements about the status of an issue or topic? What might prevent them from doing so? Is this common in literature reviews in your field? Answers to these questions may emerge at the end of all the Language Focus sections examining agreement and disagreement, concluding on page 72.

Language Focus: Expressing Agreement

This section provides some examples of agreement from papers that come from a few different disciplines.

1. The recently discovered copperless superconductor MgB2 [1] has attracted substantial attention. **Most researchers agree that MgB2** is a conventional sp-metal, where a combination of strong bonding and sizable density of states produces a high critical temperature within the standard theory [2, 3, and 4]. (Electrical Engineering/Solid State)

2. **The majority of the researchers believe that** the plasticity-induced crack closure [1], operating in the crack wake, is solely responsible for the observed load interaction effects. (Materials Science)

3. **There is wide consensus in the economic literature** on the fact that "the right kind" of structural reform, sound macro policies and trade liberalisation are beneficial to growth. (Economics)

4. In sum, **there is growing consensus that** task shifting, in its various forms, represents a promising strategy to strengthen the workforce to deliver HIV services [18]. (Medicine)

5. The hydrothermal growth of the quartz crystal **has been well established.** (Materials Science)

6. **It is widely accepted that** protection against pneumococcal AOM is more difficult to achieve than protection against invasive infections. (Immunology)

7. The importance of an intact immune system in the BCG antitumor **activity is broadly accepted** [5]. (Medicine)

Questions on Expressing Agreement

1. Can you think of any other expressions that you could use to express agreement? Could you, for instance, use the expression *the literature* as in *there is agreement in the literature that . . .* ? Check your reference collection.

2. In Examples 6–7 *accepted* is modified by *widely* and *broadly*. What other adverbs can be used to modify *accept?*

Language Focus: Expressing Disagreement

Of course, authors can also express disagreement, as demonstrated by these examples.

1. *There is ongoing discussion in the literature with respect to* the impact of outreach services. (Medicine)

2. The sheer number of alternative mRNA isoforms *has triggered an ongoing debate as to whether* the majority of these transcripts are generated by mistake. (Biochemistry)

3. Since Baldwin & Schultz in 1983 for the first time reported "plant–plant communication" (16), *it has been controversially debated whether* this phenomenon plays a role in nature (17–19). (Biology)

4. Thus, *it remains a subject of debate as to whether* the regulation of p53 is a biological function of 53BP1. (Biochemistry)

5. When irrigation is not feasible, plantation success can be greatly dependent upon seedling morpho-functional attributes. However, *there is no consensus* on the set of plant traits that determines establishment success in water-limited environments, or on the nursery methodologies needed to achieve these traits (Cortina et al., 2006). (Environmental Science)

6. *There is no agreement in the field on* a single set of criteria for Mild Cognitive Impairment (MCI). (Psychology)

7. *Some of the most respected economists in the world disagree as to* the impacts of globalization. (Economics)

8. *Geologists today still disagree as to whether* the extinction of the dinosaurs was sudden or gradual, that is, whether dinosaurs had been in decline before the K-T boundary or whether they all died suddenly at that time. (Paleontology)

9. *There is longstanding disagreement on whether* phosphorylation of Ser473 is a prerequisite for phosphorylation of Thr308 or Thr308 phosphorylation is independent of Ser473. (Cell Biology)

Questions on Expressing Disagreement

1. Which, if any, of the expressions might be appropriate for your field?

2. Can you think of any other expressions that you could use to express disagreement? Check your reference collection.

Although we have provided only a few examples here, you will notice that when commenting on researchers' perspectives, you have a lot of options. You may

- use present tense *(Geologists disagree that . . . / X is a subject of debate . . .)*
- use present perfect *(It has been debated whether . . . /X has triggered debate . . .)*
- use *there* or *it* in subject position *(There is disagreement as to whether . . . / It is widely accepted that . . .)*
- use active voice with or without mention of researchers *(Researchers agree that . . . /There is consensus that . . .)*
- use passive voice with no *by*-phrase *(It is believed that . . . / X is broadly accepted)*

Questions on Active and Passive Voice

1. When do you think active or passive might be preferred?

2. Do you think active or passive would be more common in introductions in your field? If you are not sure, look at a few introductions from your reference collection. Compare what you find to your own writing.

Language Focus: Expressing Agreement and Disagreement

Finally, many authors point to both agreement and disagreement in the field, emphasizing that certain questions have largely been settled, while others have not. In doing so, authors show an awareness of the work in their fields. More important, this may help authors open a gap for their own contribution. In your field, how important is it for you to refer to both agreement and disagreement?

1. **While there is general agreement on the top journals there is considerable disagreement** lower down. (Information Science)

2. **While archaeologists generally agree that the vessels had a ritual use, they disagree** about the nature of this ritual and the specific use of the vessels in ritual (6–8). (Archeology)

3. **Although there is still widespread disagreement over** the precise way in which this mechanism works, **most models** of word production **have shared the assumption that** lexical selection is a competitive process (Starreveld & La Heij, 1996; Levelt et al., 1999; but see Dell, 1986; Caramazza & Hillis, 1990). (Linguistics)

4. In short, **despite different assumptions about** the purposes of schooling, the nature of teaching as an enterprise, and appropriate ways to measure teaching effectiveness, **there is enormous consensus that** teaching quality makes a significant difference in learning and school effectiveness. (Education)

5. Low Vitamin D status 1 is extremely common (1, 2, 3, 4), and may contribute to the development of osteoporosis and osteomalacia/rickets, as well as increase the risk for falls (5, 6). Moreover, low Vitamin D status may play a role in nonmusculoskeletal diseases, including a variety of cancers, multiple sclerosis, infection, hypertension, and diabetes mellitus (7, 8). **Although it is widely accepted that** Vitamin D status is determined by the measurement of the circulating concentration of 25-hydroxyvitamin D [25(OH)D] (9), the cutoff value to define low Vitamin D status and a definition for success of Vitamin D repletion therapy **remain controversial** (10, 11). (Endocrinology)

6. ***Many researchers agree that*** the function of the prefrontal cortex (PFC) is broadly one of "executive control" (i.e., the scheduling and optimizing of subsidiary processes implemented by posterior cortical and subcortical regions; see [1] for a review). ***There is, however, theoretical controversy over whether*** subregions of PFC are functionally differentiated. (Cognitive Science)

7. ***Most youth researchers agree that*** risk-taking is part of the developmental make-up of adolescence. Some see it as mainly linked to harmful consequences such as bad health (Spruijt-Metz, 1999), low self-esteem and depression (Gullone, Paul, & Moore, 2000), and presenting a danger to others (Bell & Bell, 1992). ***However, in recent years, some researchers have pointed out that*** risk behaviours may fulfill positive functions in the transition to adulthood (Ciairano, 2004; Dworkin, 2005; Hendry & Kloep, 2003; Lightfoot, 1997; Ponton, 1997). (Psychology)

Questions on Expressing Both Agreement and Disagreement

1. Which logical connectors seem important for expressing agreement and disagreement within the same paragraph or sentence? How would you choose your connector if you wanted to use one?

2. How would you decide the order of the agreement or disagreement in a sentence?

3. Would you include researchers in your statements, as in Examples 6 and 7, or should you omit them, as in Examples 1 and 4?

4. Verbs like *agree* and *accept* and nouns like *agreement* are generally followed by a *that*-clause in which *that* is included. Look at all of the examples in the Language Focus. What other verbs and nouns also follow this pattern?

5. Look at your reference collection. Can you find any instances where the authors point to both agreement and disagreement?

Now that we have explored agreement and disagreement, in this next task we would like you to try a bit of writing.

Task Twenty-Three

How might you reformulate this sentence using some of the other ways of expressing agreement and disagreement? Try to come up with two versions.

> In short, *despite different assumptions about* the purposes of schooling, the nature of teaching as an enterprise, and appropriate ways to measure teaching effectiveness, *there is enormous consensus that* teaching quality makes a significant difference in learning and school effectiveness.

Establishing Your Stance

It used to be claimed that academic writing is impersonal and simply a matter of objectively reporting facts. However, the four Language Focus sections on pages 67–72, together with research have demonstrated that writers are interested in conveying their stance,[10] attitude, or perspective toward the work in their fields. By revealing both what you *know* and what you *think*, you increase the chances that your readers will see the value of your work in the same way that you do.

Apart from agreement and disagreement, many other perspectives can be conveyed. We offer a few examples to illustrate.

> Previous work has *clearly* shown that the applied stress ratio R is not equal to the stress ratio affecting the crack growth in the metallic layers.
>
> *The author has no doubt.*

> Recent work [15b] and [15c] has *elegantly* described the antioxidative properties of galanthamine and the resulting enhancement of its neuroprotective capability by lowering exposure to oxidative injury.
>
> *The author is impressed by how well this was done.*

> These studies have *greatly contributed* to our understanding of apoptosis and have raised *interesting* questions that await further clarification.
>
> *The author sees these studies as important.*

---

[10]Your textual voice; your personal stamp of authority in relation to a text (Hyland, 2005).

Authors may have a lot to consider as they try to find just the right way to express their stance—but this is not apparent when we read. To illustrate the challenge, let's take a look at these two sentences.

1. A significant limitation of this approach is the time needed to do the calculations.

2. A potential drawback of this approach is the time needed to do the calculations.

Sentence 1 was written by one of our students for a paper that introduces a new method to support the ship design process. This process is significantly faster and less expensive than currently used methods. As you may have guessed, the sentence is part of Move 2 in the introduction where the student is attempting to establish a gap in the research by referring to a limitation that is well known in his field. The student's advisor, however, commented that Sentence 1 should be rewritten and gave Sentence 2 as an alternative. Can you guess why?

The advisor explained that it is important to consider the potential impact of an overly strong statement. The advisor further stated that, while the limitation of the current approach is well known, the current method was developed by some very well established members of the field. Thus, describing the weakness as *significant* would reflect poorly on the student (and the advisor as co-author). Would you agree?

Your perspective can be revealed in any of the moves in an RA introduction, but the scope of your evaluative commentary may vary depending on the move. For instance, in Move 1 you may indicate your stance toward the general topic, while in Move 2 you may focus more on the research itself. In Move 3, your stance toward your own work can be revealed. Read through these examples. The authors' stance is highlighted in bold.

Move 1: Melon is enjoyed worldwide as a delicious dessert fruit. There are a **great** number of varieties of melon with an **astonishing** range of biological characteristics.[1]

Move 2: Up to 1992, 257 compounds have been identified in melon fruit.[13] Although the volatile components of melon have been delineated in many **excellent** studies [9,12,14–19], few sensory investigations have been carried out using GC–O.[20–25]

Move 3: In this study we describe the chemical (GC–MS) and sensorial (GC–O, AEDA) analysis of a honeydew melon hydrodistillate extract. We strived to utilize a **state-of-the-art yet practical** approach by employing recent improvements in natural product isolation, trace chemical analysis and character impact determination.

Your stance toward the literature can be revealed in several ways, some subtle and some obvious. In this example, some of the stance expressions are highlighted in bold.

① Counterfeiting, the production and sale of illegal, low-priced, and often lower-quality replicas of goods which seem identical to the original product, has been spreading across the globe at an **alarming** rate (Lai & Zaichkowsky, 1999). ② **Preferred** targets of counterfeiters are products which carry a high brand image and require a **relatively** simple production technology, such as wearing apparel, consumer electronics, media, cigarettes, watches and toys (International Anti-Counterfeiting Coalition, 2002). ③ Manufacturers of the original products are **well** aware of these developments and leave no opportunity untapped to limit damages to their company's brand reputation and profits (e.g., Green & Smith, 2002; Kay, 1990; Nash, 1989; Wee, Tan, & Cheok, 1995).

Task Twenty-Four

Underline the language in these excerpts that seems to indicate a perspective. The first text revisits the counterfeiting topic on page 75.

① The global market for counterfeits today is estimated to exceed $600 billion, accounting for approximately 7% of world trade (World Customs Organization, 2004). ② The ethical case against counterfeiting aside, its adverse effects on business are well documented and many. ③ For example, the U.S. Chamber of Commerce (2006) holds counterfeiting responsible for the loss of more than 750,000 U.S. jobs per year. ④ Perhaps more dire, counterfeiting has also been linked to the growing global threats of narcotics, weapons, human trafficking, and terrorism (Thomas, 2007). ⑤ Not surprisingly, companies are allying with governments and enforcement agencies to devote unprecedented resources to tackle this global problem (International AntiCounterfeiting Coalition, 2008).

⑥ The academic literature displays a strong focus on the supply side, while the demand side—why consumers buy fake products—has been badly neglected. ⑦ Even if companies and governments manage to restrict the supply of fake products, counterfeiters have consistently demonstrated their abilities to find new ways to serve customers, as long as the demand is still thriving (Albers-Miller, 1999; Ang, Cheng, Lim, & Tambyah, 2001). ⑧ It appears necessary, therefore, to focus more attention on the demand side in order to gain a better understanding of what drives customers to voluntarily buy counterfeits.

⑨ Existing research on luxury goods has strongly suggested that consumers' attitudes toward luxury brands may in fact have a social-adjustive function.

If you are in engineering and the hard sciences, you may question whether stance should play a role in your writing. To help you explore this matter, read through this text and identify the expressions that appear to indicate the writer's stance.

1. Introduction

① Semiconductor lasers are typical devices for information transmission in optical communications using direct modulation. ② At the present time, stable single-mode diode lasers with a very short pulse width, low chirp and high speed modulation capability are highly desirable to prevent pulse variance in the Haul telecommunication system. ③ Unfortunately, a communication system using a high speed direct modulation is limited by relaxation oscillations which result from the interplay between the optical field and the free-carrier density [1].

④ Nowadays, there is considerable interest in compact laser sources that operate in the blue region at picosecond pulse duration for different applications in science and technology. ⑤ The frequency doubling of near-infrared diode lasers with a waveguided antireflection coating nonlinear crystal (second harmonic generation element) represents a competitive methodology for obtaining a compact blue light source. ⑥ In spite of the wide applications of the IFD of a Q-switched diode laser, they still up to now are under consideration [2].

⑦ The KTP crystal can be periodically poled to satisfy quasi-phase-matching conditions that increase the second harmonic (SH) conversion efficiency at room temperature for a pulsed lasers [3, 4]. ⑧ Different methods are widely used to generate stable single-mode very short optical pulses including mode-locking, Q-switching and gain switching. ⑨ Excellent thermal quality, chemical stability and high optical nonlinearity make GaAs an ideal semiconductor saturable absorber for the passive Q-switching process. ⑩ The bandgap of the GaAs saturable absorber is about 1.42 eV (figure 1).

As the engineering example indicates, you can reveal your perspective, regardless of your field or claims by others that academic writing is entirely objective.

Task Twenty-Five

Look back at the examples of agreement and disagreement on pages 67–71, and find the expressions that strengthen or weaken (hedge) the verbs and nouns and thus may help indicate a stance. Using your reference articles, expand the table with some of your own examples of other verbs and nouns along with other possible language that strengthens or softens a claim. The first verb, *accept*, has been done for you.

Modifiers that Strengthen	Modifiers that Soften	Verbs	Modifiers that Strengthen	Modifiers that Soften	Nouns
widely, broadly		accept	widespread	some	acceptance
		agree			agreement
		debate			debate
		disagree			disagreement
					discussion
					controversy
					consensus
					researchers
		believe			
		establish			

Reference Collection Examples

Modifiers that Strengthen	Modifiers that Weaken	Verbs	Modifiers that Strengthen	Modifiers that Weaken	Nouns

Highlighting the Need for Research: The Gap

Your introduction opening, chosen citations, and stance should together tell a good research story that has the cumulative effect of creating a space for the research you have done (Move 2). Although this space can be created in a number of ways, as suggested in Table 2 (see page 55), one possibility is to indicate a clear gap in the research, as demonstrated in these examples.

> *Despite the interest in this area, there has yet to be a study that examines* the effects of both the pay-performance and the market for corporate control theories simultaneously.

> *Unfortunately, previous work has not furnished* an answer or the material for an answer to this important question.

> *However, no study has adequately explored the possibility that* there may be an assortment of physical ideals represented in the media, which may vary according to the different audiences being targeted.

> *While several studies have looked into the issue of* arsenic contamination, *most existing studies* ([Chakraborti and Saha, 1987], [Das et al., 1994], [Das et al., 1996], [Dang et al., 1983], [Garai et al., 1984], [Guha Mazumdar et al., 1984], [Guha Mazumdar et al., 1988], [Guha Mazumder et al., 1998], [Guha Mazumder et al., 2000] and [Guha Mazumdar, 2001]) *explore* the geological and climate features, the scale of the problem in terms of population coverage, the intensity and variety of health problems, and the technologies for arsenic removal. *None of the studies cited above addresses* the economic dimension to welfare loss and hence the associated costs and benefits of arsenic contamination and removal.

One study of Move 2s in computer science RAs (Shehzad, 2008) provides some interesting results to consider when establishing a gap. First, although a variety of adversative connectors (e.g., *although* and *however*) may be employed to signal a gap, in computer science RAs *however* is strongly preferred, as in other fields. (See Table 5.)

Table 5. Logical Connectors in Gapping (N = 77)

Connector	N	Percentage
however	36	47
while	14	18
but	11	14
although	11	14
nevertheless	1	1
other	4	5
	77	99.00

(Percentages have been rounded. Data from Shehzad [2008].)

The use of logical connectors, however, is not obligatory. Second, as you may have already observed in the arsenic example given earlier, gapping can involve several sentences. In some computer science RAs, for instance, the majority of the introduction may be devoted to Move 2. Third, there may be disciplinary preferences for the type of gap, whether the gap is strongly negative or not.

Rather than pointing to the absence of research in Move 2, another possibility is to indicate that there is a need or opportunity to expand the body of existing research. Move 2s of this type may be more common in some fields than in others. In computer science, for instance, less than five percent of RAs employ this type of Move 2 (Shehzad, 2008).

The number of published studies that examined these important personal characteristics *is small, pointing to the need for further investigation into* ways to best address diverse patient needs across the health care continuum.

What is therefore needed is a high-resolution magnetic encoder system that overcomes the disadvantages of the prior systems.

The completion of rice genome sequencing (Goff et al., 2002; Yu et al., 2002) *thus allows us to study* the function of the rice U-box proteins at the genome scale. By using a battery of extensive whole genome analysis algorithms, we identify 77 genes encoding U-box domain-containing proteins.

Because of the large carbon storage capacity and potential for its release in the form of carbon dioxide or methane, *it is clear that a logical next step* in terms of modeling the carbon cycle *is* the integration of peatlands into coupled carbon–climate models.

In this next task we consider an introduction that emphasizes adding to the existing research as opposed to highlighting an absence of research.

Task Twenty-Six

Read this nearly complete introduction from the field of finance. All of the sentences are given except for the one indicating that the research is an extension of previous work. After reading Sentences 1–7, consider which, if any, of the given options is the best Sentence 8.

Herding and Information Based Trading
Rhea Tingyu Zhoua and Rose Neng Lai

① This paper tests the coexistence of two types of phenomena: herding and informational cascades. ② With herding, people tend to crowd together with others, making identical investment decisions. ③ This is especially common in markets having less publicly available information. ④ This well-known phenomenon has been widely studied over the last two decades. ⑤ According to Bikhchandani et al. (1992), individuals with access to information that is less accurate tend to follow the lead of individuals that have access to information that is more accurate than their own. ⑥ Ignoring their own information, such individuals tend to form herds, with the best informed individuals making their decisions first. ⑦ These decision makers are known as "fashion leaders," and the phenomenon hence known as "informational cascades."

⑧ _____

_____. ⑨ We start by testing if

herding takes place in the market. ⑩ If so, we examine if informational

asymmetry exists within the herding process.

⑧ⓐ Do informational cascades, in fact, cause part of the herding phenomenon?

⑧ⓑ It would therefore be of interest to know whether informational

cascades do, in fact, cause part of the herding phenomenon.

⑧ⓒ It is therefore crucial to examine this issue.

⑧ⓓ This then raises the question as to whether and to what extent

informational cascades are in fact responsible for herding.

⑧ⓔ No additional sentence needed—just move to Sentence 9.

Task Twenty-Six has demonstrated that a strong negative gap is not necessary to justify the research that will be presented. Instead, the need for the
research can be indicated by establishing a causal connection as in 8a or 8d.
In some introductions there seems to be little justification for the research—
as if to suggest that anyone reading the background would see the value in
the work being presented. In such introductions, after describing what has
been done previously, the authors announce what they did. Our students tell
us that introductions of this type are relatively common in papers in epidemiology and those in various engineering fields, but they can be found in
other fields as well such as psychology and education. We might label this
kind of Move 2 as *continuing the research strand.*

Task Twenty-Seven ▬▬▬▬▬▬▬▬▬▬▬▬▬▬

By this time we hope you are able to identify and label the different moves of an introduction. Read the introduction from materials science, and answer the questions at the end. Note that in the journal *Applied Physics Letters*, papers are referred to as letters.

Sicot, M., Bouvron, S., Zander, O., Rüdiger, U., Dedkov, S. and Fonin, M. (2010). Nucleation and growth of nickel nanoclusters on graphene Moiré on Rh(111). *Applied Physics Letters*, *96(9)*, 093115-1–093115-3.

① The development of advanced routes to fabricate highly ordered monodispersed metallic nanostructures is one of the key challenges in modern nanotechnology. ② Transition metal nanoclusters (NCs) have become of special scientific interest and technological importance since they exhibit unique electronic structure, size-dependent catalytic activity, and selectivity as well as magnetic properties that are distinctly different from the bulk. [1] ③ One of the promising ways to produce arrays of homogeneously distributed monodispersed NCs is to use a bottom-up approach where self-organization growth phenomena on template substrates are used. ④ So far, regular arrays of NCs were assembled using surfaces such as alumina double layers on Ni3A [1,2,3] vicinal Au(111) surfaces, [4,5] reconstructed surfaces [6,7] or h-BN nanomesh. [8,9] ⑤ Recently, graphene Moiré on close-packed metal surfaces like Pt(111),10 Rh(111),11 Ru(0001), [12,13] and Ir(111) [14,15] has been suggested to be a good candidate for the templated growth of clusters arrays. ⑥ Recent works demonstrate that superlattices of metallic clusters of Re, W, Pt, and Ir on such graphene Moiré can be realized effectively. [15,16,17,18]

⑦ In this letter, we report on the growth of nanometer-sized Ni clusters on graphene Moiré on Rh(111). ⑧ Growth and organization of Ni NCs deposited at different temperatures are investigated by means of scanning tunneling microscopy (STM) at room temperature

(RT). ⑨ Although Ni NCs deposited at 150 K and at low coverage are homogeneously sized and adsorbed on well-defined sites, no regular arrays exhibiting a long-range order could be obtained upon increasing the surface coverage. ⑩ For RT deposition, the formation of flat triangular-shaped Ni islands is observed.

1. What is the purpose of the first paragraph?

2. What is the aim of the second paragraph? What kind of detail is offered?

3. Can you find any instances where the authors reveal their perspective?

4. In Sentence 7, can you think of any other verbs besides *report on* that could be used?

5. What verb tenses are used in Sentences 3–6? Why do you suppose these verb forms were used?

6. In the second paragraph does active or passive voice predominate? What seems to have motivated the choice of voice?

Filling the Gap

At the end of the introduction, readers may reasonably expect to see what your specific contribution to the research is as well as some text organizing features that give a preview or indicate an action (Skulstad, 2005). This can be accomplished in one of these ways.

1. A global preview in which you state your purpose

   The aim of this paper is to . . .

2. An action marker in which you state what you do or your paper does

   Here we explain a new method that . . .

   This paper describes the mechanisms underlying . . .

3. A local preview in which you give an overview of the organization of distinct parts of your paper

   Section One discusses . . . Section Two details . . .

Task Twenty-Eight

Here are two examples of Move 3 overviews. Read them, and consider the questions after the excerpts.

A. The paper is organized as follows. Section 2 presents the main features of the FRACTAL model. Section 3 describes JULIA, a Java framework that supports the FRACTAL model. Section 4 evaluates the model and its supporting framework. Section 5 discusses related work. Section 6 concludes the paper with some indications for future work.

B. The remainder of this paper is organized as follows. In Section 2 we review the data and present some summary statistics. Section 3 presents the results of analyses that relate probability of sale of individuals' mutual fund investments with a range of fund characteristics, including past performance, determinants of future potential tax liabilities, and investment costs. In Section 4 we aggregate investors' buys and sells of mutual funds into monthly measures of inflows and outflows, and analyze the determinants of those flows. Section 5 concludes.

1. Text A begins with *the paper*, while B begins with *this paper*. Do you have a preference for one over the other? Does *the paper* seem to have a different effect on you as a reader compared to *this paper*? Why?

2. In Text B the authors include themselves using *we*. Text A, on the other hand, anthropomorphizes (i.e., attributes human activities to), the sections. Which do you prefer? Why?

3. What words or expressions do the texts have in common? Could you use these in your own writing?

4. How much variety in the sentence structure of the two overviews do you notice? How important is it to vary the sentence structure to create interest?

5. Do you think that this version represents an improvement of Text A?

The paper is organized as follows. Section 2 presents the main features of the FRACTAL model, while Section 3 describes JULIA, a Java framework that supports the FRACTAL model. The model together with its supporting framework is evaluated in Section 4, followed by Section 5, which discusses related work. Finally, the paper concludes in Section 6 with some indications for future work.

Language Focus: Guiding Your Readers

The language used to provide an overview or indicate the purpose of your work is a special type of language commonly referred to as **metadiscourse.** Numerous definitions of metadiscourse have been proposed over the years, leading to quite a lot of ambiguity and disagreement (Hyland, 2005). Much of the ongoing debate has to do with what constitutes metadiscourse. Some scholars, such as Hyland, take a rather broad view, while others, notably Swales, take a more narrow view. This lack of agreement makes it difficult to offer clear guidance to authors as to how and whether to employ metadiscourse in academic writing. To avoid this, here we have chosen to avoid the disagreement and instead focus on how authors can guide readers through a text. We follow Hyland's thinking and maintain that guiding readers involves making your ideas and content "coherent, intelligible, and persuasive to a particular audience" (Hyland, 2005). Thus, guiding readers might require you to reveal organization (e.g., **this paper offers three arguments regarding . . .**) as well as your attitude (e.g., **surprisingly no study has examined . . .**). Incorporating both of these elements can contribute to the creation of a well-written and well-argued paper.

Hyland (2005) offers a perspective that follows Thompson (2001) in categorizing guidance into two types: interactive (organizational) and interactional (attitudinal). As described in Table 6, organizational language is chosen by authors to take control over the flow of information to reveal their organizational interpretations of that information. This would include, for example, roadmaps, as described earlier, and the use of logical connectors to show the relationship between ideas. Attitudinal language, on the one hand, is chosen by authors to reveal their relationship with or perspective on their content. For example, language that strengthens or weakens a claim, such as that described earlier on pages 73–75, can be considered interactional. A summary of these categories based on Hyland is provided in Table 6.

Table 6. Types of Language for Guiding Readers Based on Hyland (2005)

Category	Function	Examples
Organizational Purpose: to guide readers through the text		
Transitions*	express meaning relationships between main clauses	*in addition, but, thus, and*
Frame markers	announce what the author is doing	*finally, to conclude, my purpose is to*
Text internal links	refer to information in other parts of the text	*noted above, see Fig., in Section 2*
Text external links	refer to source of information from other texts	*according to AUTHOR, (AUTHOR, 2010), AUTHOR (2010) states*
Clarifications	help readers grasp meanings of points	*namely, e.g., such as, in other words*
Attitudinal		
Purpose: to involve the reader in the text		
Hedges	withhold writer's full commitment to a point	*might, perhaps, possible, about*
Boosters	emphasize force or writer's certainty regarding a point	*in fact, definitely, it is clear that*
Attitude markers	express writer's attitude toward the proposition	*unfortunately, I agree, surprisingly*
Engagement markers	explicitly refer to or build relationship with reader	*consider, note that, you can see that*
Self-mentions	explicit reference to author(s)	*I, we, my, our*

*Note that there is disagreement as to whether these should be considered as forms of metadiscourse. These are, however, ways to help direct readers and thus include them here.

Of the specific types of guiding language, transitions and hedges tend to be the most common in graduate student writing, but all types are used to varying degrees.

Task Twenty-Nine

Examine your reference collection of RA introductions again, and identify the language that guides or directs the reader. You have already done some of this task if you answered Questions 4 and 8 in Task Twenty.

Problem-Focused Introductions

Another approach to organizing your introduction is one that focuses on real problems that need to be addressed. The difference between problem-focused introductions and gap-focused introductions is that problems involve difficulties that the author believes should be solved (but have not been despite research or interest), while gaps highlight the absence of research. As with CaRS introductions, problem-focused introductions contextualize the need for the research within the larger body of previous work. Different from the classic CaRS introductions, problem-focused introductions highlight the need for their contribution to the research by explaining a problem with a circumstance or set of circumstances, which may or may not emerge from existing research. We deal with problem-focused introductions separately here because they are more prevalent than gap-focused introductions in some fields such as law.

This next text comes from a paper focusing on the right of publicity (the right to control the use of one's name, image, likeness, or other aspects of one's identity for money-making purposes). An *n* followed by a number is a reference to a footnote, a very common feature of academic legal writing. Footnotes have various functions, but often they provide a citation to a source. For ease of reading, however, we have omitted the notes. We have indicated the different moves to the right of the text.

2006 *Journal of Law and Policy*, 14, 471–523
Adjudicating the Right of Publicity in Three Easy Steps
David M. Schlachter

Introduction

① Celebrities' names, images, and identities are unique and valuable entities. n1 ② The right of publicity was created to protect these entities. ③ While celebrities usually have wealth, fame, and prestige, they also have the right of publicity to protect their personas. ④ This additional advantage is warranted because celebrities have a set of heightened property and privacy interests in their personas. n2 ⑤ The right of publicity, therefore, makes it unlawful to misappropriate a valuable identity without permission. n3

Background situation with references

⑥ Courts have historically struggled to define the right of publicity. ⑦ This difficulty is apparent in inconsistent approaches to defining the right. n4 ⑧ Without a firm definition of the right of publicity, courts are left to question its necessity, how far the right should extend, and who may bring a cause of action under the right's authority. ⑨ Furthermore, issues such as whether the right of publicity is derived from privacy or property jurisprudence, and whether the First Amendment right to freedom of expression serves to limit or expand the right of publicity, also contribute to the confusion surrounding this right. ⑩ Such uncertainty has led courts to apply varying and divergent methods of adjudicating a right of publicity cause of action. ⑪ Therefore, both plaintiffs and defendants are left with little guidance on how to litigate cases which deal with the right of publicity.

Description of the problem

⑫ The purpose of this Note is to untangle the right of publicity and annunciate its defining issues. ⑬ Part I explains the right's foundation and the various privacy and property interests that the right of publicity protects. ⑭ Part II discusses the interaction of the right of publicity with the First Amendment, explaining how varying degrees of First Amendment protection act as a restraint on the right of publicity. ⑮ Part III highlights the necessity of a new uniform test and examines flaws in current right of publicity jurisprudence, reflecting a lack of understanding of the right that leads to confusion and injustice.

Addressing the problem

⑯ Finally, Part IV suggests a new three-prong test to consistently adjudicate right of publicity actions and applies the new test to several fact patterns for illustrative purposes.

Proposed solution to the problem

As demonstrated by the example, problem-focused introductions have several moves. In fact, they have as many as five.

Move 1: Establishing the background

Move 2: Highlighting a problem that has emerged

Move 3: Outlining how the problem will be examined

Move 4: Proposed solution to the problem (optional, but likely)

Move 5: Outlining the paper (optional)

This next task provides another example of a problem-focused introduction, this time from engineering.

Task Thirty

Read this introduction, and answer the questions.

Efficient Model Checking of Applications with Input/Output

Artho Cyrille, Boris Zweimuller, Armin Biere,
Etsuya Shibayama, and Shinichi Honiden

① Model checking explores the entire behavior of a system under test (SUT) by investigating each reachable system state [5] for different thread schedules. ② Recently, model checking has been applied directly to software [2,4,6,7,13]. ③ However, conventional software model checking techniques are not applicable to networked programs. ④ The problem is that state space exploration involves backtracking. ⑤ After backtracking, the model checker will execute certain parts of the program (and thus certain input/output operations) again. ⑥ However, external processes, which are not under the control of the model checking engine, cannot be kept in synchronization with backtracking, causing direct communication between the SUT and external processes to fail. ⑦ Our work proposes a solution to this problem. ⑧ It covers all input/output (I/O) operations on streams and is applicable as long as I/O operations of the SUT always produce the same data stream, regardless of the non-determinism of the schedule.

⑨ This paper is organized as follows. An intuition for our algorithm is given in Section 2, while Section 3 formalizes our algorithm. ⑩ Experiments are given in Section 4. Section 5 describes related work. ⑪ Future work is outlined in Section 6, which concludes this paper.

Artho, C., Zweimuller, B., Biere, A., Shibayama, E., and Honiden. S. (2007). Efficient Model Checking of Applications with Input/Output. In *Proceedings of Computer Aided Systems Theory (EUROCAST'07), Lecture Notes in Computer Science, 4739*, 515–522.

1. Which sentences contribute to the five moves?

   Move 1: _____

   Move 2: _____

   Move 3: _____

   Move 4: _____

   Move 5: _____

2. Why do you suppose the authors used *however* to begin Sentence 3?

3. The authors clearly identify the problem by saying *the problem is that*. Can you think of any alternatives to this phrase?

4. Sentence 8 begins with *it*. What do you think of the use of *it* here? Could the authors have been more clear?

5. This introduction ends with a roadmap or outline of the paper, as does the right of publicity introduction. Would you make any changes to it?

When we introduced the right to publicity introduction in a research paper writing class, several of our students thought that the first paragraph could be improved. They said that although they understood the paragraph well enough, it did require some effort. Here, we offer some of that class discussion of one group of students (Jin, Sam, Jay, Claudia, and Sergio). We begin by providing the first paragraph of the introduction as a starting point.

① Celebrities' names, images, and identities are unique and valuable entities. n1 ② The right of publicity was created to protect these entities. ③ While celebrities usually have wealth, fame, and prestige, they also have the right of publicity to protect their personas. ④ This additional advantage is warranted because celebrities have a set of heightened property and privacy interests in their personas. n2 ⑤ The right of publicity, therefore, makes it unlawful to misappropriate a valuable identity without permission. n3

Jin: I don't see a strong connection between Sentence 1 and Sentence 2. *The right of publicity* comes from nowhere. But the end of the sentence gives the connection when it says *these entities*. I don't think that is a good connection.

Sam: So, maybe it could be rewritten to tie it together better. (Students worked on rewriting and the group offers Text A as a revision.)

A. ① Celebrities' names, images, and identities are unique and valuable entities. n1 ② To protect these entities the courts created the right of publicity. ③ While celebrities usually have wealth, fame, and prestige, they also have the right of publicity to protect their personas. ④ This additional advantage is warranted because celebrities have a set of heightened property and privacy interests in their personas. n2 ⑤ The right of publicity, therefore, makes it unlawful to misappropriate a valuable identity without permission. n3

Jay: This one (Text A) is better, but if you fix Sentences 1 and 2, you have to look at the next sentences, too. Sentence 3 now jumps back to celebrities, and it doesn't sound good. Something is missing.

Claudia: Right. It seems that you need to say something about the right. So, just like before you can move the information around. (Students worked on rewriting again and the group offers Text B as a revision.)

B. ① Celebrities' names, images, and identities are unique and valuable entities. n1 ② To protect these entities the courts created the right of publicity. ③ This right gives celebrities a means to protect their personas, which are tied to their wealth, fame, and prestige. ④ This additional right is warranted because celebrities have a set of heightened property and privacy interests in their personas. n2 ⑤ The right of publicity, therefore, makes it unlawful to misappropriate a valuable identity without permission. n3

Jin: I think the text needs more work to be clear and maybe some vocabulary can be changed. Why does it say *additional right?* What does it mean? Maybe it should say *special right?* Not everyone has it, so it's special, isn't it?

Sergio: Okay, yes, that makes sense. So, we can make that change. But what about saying something about why those celebrities are special? Why do they need some special right? Why is there *heightened interest?*

Sam: I think it's probably because they can make money from their names. You know, from just being some kind of celebrity, even if they haven't done much. Like those people on TV dancing shows where the celebrities that aren't really celebrities compete against each other.

Jay: So, can we add that? That they make money from just being a celebrity? (Students worked on rewriting again and the group offers Text C as a revision.)

    C. ① Celebrities' names, images, and identities are unique and valuable entities. n1 ② To protect these entities the courts created the right of publicity. ③ This right gives celebrities a means to protect their personas, which are tied to their wealth, fame, and prestige. ④ This special right is warranted because a persona is viewed as something that a celebrity owns, not unlike a piece of property, and is a means to further monetary and non-monetary gains. ⑤ Thus, different from an average person, celebrities have a set of heightened property and privacy interests in their personas. n2 ⑥ The right of publicity, therefore, makes it unlawful to misappropriate a valuable identity without permission. n3

Jin: This (Text C) looks a lot better. But, don't you think the last sentence now seems like it should be better connected? All you have to do is start with something like *these interests* to capture the end of Sentence 5.

Claudia: That makes sense. Let's try that. (Students rewrite and produce Text D.)

D. ① Celebrities' names, images, and identities are unique and valuable entities. n1 ② To protect these entities the courts created the right of publicity. ③ This right gives celebrities a means to protect their personas, which are tied to their wealth, fame, and prestige. ④ This special right is warranted because a persona is viewed as something that a celebrity owns, not unlike a piece of property, and is a means to further monetary and non-monetary gains. ⑤ Thus, different from an average person, celebrities have a set of heightened property and privacy interests in their personas. n2 ⑥ These interests have been recognized by the courts as the right of publicity, which makes it unlawful to misappropriate a valuable identity without permission. n3

Task Thirty-One

What is your reaction to the revision process? Do you think Text D reflects good improvements to Text A?

Specific-General Introductions in the Humanities

Although most introductions move from more general topics to more specific ones, exceptions to this pattern can be found in fields such as history, literature, and fine art. Writers in these areas sometimes begin with a specific historical event, a few lines of poetry, or a single work of art and use that as a way of moving on toward some broader theme. As Bondi (2007) suggests, these types of openings offer the reader "immediate contact with the object of study." An example of this can be found in art history introductions, in which, according to Tucker (2003), the opening section is expected to offer a description of the work that can "guide and coordinate the interpretative demonstration" that will follow.

A further characteristic of art history article introductions is that they typically lack explicit markers of moves and steps as described in the CaRS model (Tucker, 2003). To gain a better understanding of how authors enact a specific to general introduction, read the introduction in Task Thirty-One, which discusses a Danish print.

Task Thirty-Two

Read the introductions, and answer the questions at the end.

Peter Ilsted (1861–1933) and Wilhelm Hammershøi (1864–1916)

① The illustration shows a 1915 colored mezzotint by the Danish artist Peter Ilsted, who is an acknowledged master of this difficult reproductive technique. ② It was entitled *Girl with a Tray* and shows a young woman about to enter an upstairs bedroom carrying a tray containing a water carafe and two glasses. ③ To modern eyes, it might appear that the dress of the young woman would indicate that she was either a housemaid or a nurse, but studies of early 20th century Danish clothing (e.g., Frandsen, 1984) establish that such long white cotton dresses were the typical clothes of middle class women of that time and place. ④ As Ilsted often used his own children as models, the *Girl with a Tray* is probably one of his daughters.

⑤ Peter Ilsted was the brother-in-law and neighbor of Wilhelm Hammershøi, a world-class painter of portraits and interior scenes, whose work is now represented in many famous art galleries. ⑥ Both he and Ilsted were leading representatives of what is sometimes called the Copenhagen School, which focused on depicting quiet interiors of middle-class city homes. ⑦ Donson, who prepared an exhibition catalogue of Ilsted's mezzotints, characterized the work of the School as "Sunshine and Silent Rooms" (Donson, 1991). ⑧ By 1915, however, Hammershøi's productive career was essentially over as he was terminally ill with throat cancer, so it is possible that the mezzotint shows one of Hammershøi's nieces bringing water for his diseased throat.

⑨ Although this last observation must remain a speculation, in more general terms much is known about the personal relations between Ilsted and Hammershøi and their families. ⑩ What is less clear are the historical influences that shaped the distinctive art of the Copenhagen School. ⑪ It is, therefore, the purpose of this paper to try and throw some further light on this important episode in the history of northern European art. ⑫ In particular, I will examine the likely influence on both Danish artists of 17th century Dutch painters, such as Vermeer.

1. Art history article introductions may be organized in this manner.

    description of a single work of art

    placement of that work in its historical context

    broader interpretation/explanations

    To what extent does the *Girl with a Tray* introduction follow this pattern?

2. Where in the introduction does the author hedge or cautiously state his claims? Does this seem necessary? Why?

3. In the third paragraph the author inserts himself into the introduction. Do you think it makes sense to do so in this type of introduction? Why?

4. The author briefly clarifies a central characteristic of the Copenhagen School in Sentence 6, and offers very little explanation for mezzotint in Sentence 1, saying only that it is a difficult reproductive technique. What do these choices indicate about the author's assumptions of the audience?

5. Would the specific to general organization used in this introduction be appropriate for any published RAs or other kinds of published papers in your field?

At this point, it is time for you to write your own RA introduction.

Task Thirty-Three

Write an introduction to a research paper that would be suitable for a published RA on a topic of interest to you. Your introduction can focus on actual research that you are doing or research that you would like to do.

Short Research Reports

Many straightforward research reports do not require complex introductions. Rather, they can start with a simple scene setting. This applies particularly to shorter research communications. The example that follows is taken from a small regional journal, *Michigan Birds and Natural History*, and deals with one of the most famous birds in North America, the sandhill crane. As you can see from the illustration, sandhill cranes are large, elegant birds that are easy to identify.

Task Thirty-Four

Read the introduction of the sandhill crane report, and answer the questions at the end.

Late Autumn Population of Sandhill Cranes in Michigan
Ronald H. Hoffman

① Early estimates of the Greater Sandhill Crane (*Grus canadensis tabida*) population in Michigan typically focused on counting pairs during the breeding season (Walkinshaw, 1949; Walkinshaw and Wing, 1955; Walkinshaw and Hoffman 1974; Hoffman, 1989). ② As the abundance and distribution of the sandhill crane increased (Brewer et al., 1991), it has become increasingly difficult to census cranes during the breeding season.

③ Annually, beginning in late August in the Upper Peninsula (UP) and early September farther south in the state, cranes gather at traditional staging areas prior to migration. ④ Walkinshaw (1949), Walkinshaw and Wing (1955), H. Wing (unpubl. field notes), and others made counts at individual staging areas, but no coordinated surveys were conducted in Michigan until 1979. ⑤ In 1979, an annual fall census was begun of the eastern population of cranes breeding in the Great Lakes states and southern Canada (Lovvorn and Kirkpatrick, 1981). ⑥ After the Lovvorn and Kirkpatrick (1981) report, there have been no published results of the annual fall census in Michigan.

⑦ This report documents the 1979–2008 changes in crane numbers and distribution based on fall censuses. ⑧ These parameters are important for identifying and managing areas for cranes, wildlife viewing, and photography.

Hoffman, R.H. (2009). Late autumn population of sandhill cranes in Michigan. *Michigan Birds and Natural History, 16* (2), 53–59.

1. This is a short introduction (fewer than 200 words), but it seems to come across as quite scholarly. In your view, which of these features contribute the most to this impression?

   a. the use of the Latin name in the opening sentence

   b. the many references in the first two paragraphs

   c. the avoidance of first-person pronouns

   d. the heavy use of dates to show changes and developments

   e. the use of the passive in the middle paragraph

   f. the avoidance of evaluative or subjective depictions of the cranes

2. In the last paragraph the author describes his publication as a *report*. What does this tell us? And what do you think about the choice of *documents* as a reporting verb?

3. What do you think of the final sentence in the introduction? Do you think something more specific or something stronger might have been written? What about, "Without this survey data, it becomes almost impossible to plan for . . ."?

Introductions to Proposals

There are so many different kinds of proposals, both large and small, that it is difficult to consider all the different ones that you may need to write. Common proposals for graduate students are the dissertation proposal (also referred to as a *prospectus*), proposals to fund research projects, and travel grant proposals.[11] For academics, main proposals are those for funding to undertake research. Although the purposes of these different proposals may differ, overall your aim is to convince a known or unknown reader that your research, activity, or scholarship is worth doing or funding. In other words, you are seeking approval of some form. To be successful, research proposals need to consider these central questions.

- What do you plan to do?
- Why is this work important for the field?
- How will you do the work?

As with dissertation introductions, which are discussed on pages 111-15, many kinds of proposals will adhere to the conventions for RA introductions. However, in many cases there is no single, prescribed format; in others, there are strict guidelines unique to a funding agency or an advisor, as in the case of a dissertation proposal. In the United States, dissertation proposals in some fields are increasingly expected to abide by the guidelines of major government funding agencies such as the National Institutes of Health or National Science Foundation—even in fields outside the health sciences such as education. Outside the U.S., there may be an expected format that all dissertation proposals are expected to follow, regardless of the field.

In this small volume, it is impossible to address all possible proposal formats. However, we do offer a sample of a successful NIH-style dissertation proposal introduction that was submitted by one of our graduate students to the U.S. National Institute of Nursing Research, which is part of the NIH;

---

[11] These shorter proposals for short-term funding or travel are dealt with in the volume entitled, *Navigating Academia: Writing Supporting Genres*.

the student subsequently received nearly $70,000 in funding. While this proposal may be quite different from the proposals you must write, we believe that it can reveal the kind of thinking that should go into any successful proposal introduction.

Task Thirty-Five

After the abstract, the "specific aims" is the first narrative part of the proposal, which serves as an introduction. Read through this introductory section, and then answer the questions.

① In 2008, the Centers for Medicare and Medicaid Services began implementing its landmark decision to restrict reimbursement to hospitals for the cost of preventable patient injury and infection (Centers for Medicare and Medicaid Services, 2009). ② This decision is intended to save the government billions of dollars, drive patient safety initiatives and spur healthcare reform to address medical errors. ③ The widespread impact of this decision will likely have marginal financial repercussions on the relatively rare medical injuries such as operating on the wrong limb or infusing incompatible blood. ④ However, the decision to impose a financial penalty on the more commonplace hospital-acquired patient injuries such as pressure ulcers, falls and hospital-acquired infection (HAI) will shift the traditional view of hospital complications from that of an inevitable consequence of hospitalization, to that of an entirely preventable event.

⑤ One potential focus of this reform may likely include the prevention of the HAI caused by the pathogen *Clostridium difficile* (*C. difficile*). *C. difficile*, a gram-positive, spore-forming, anaerobic bacillus that produces intestinal disease, is now the most common organism causing HAI in the United States (Dubberke et al., 2008; McDonald, Owings, & Jernigan D., 2006). ⑥ The rate of *C. difficile* infection (CDI) tripled between the years 2000-2005, without evidence of a peak or plateau (Gerding, 2008; McDonald et al., 2006). ⑦ Compounding the rising incidence of CDI, is an increase in both severity and mortality of the disease (Kelly, 2009; Redelings MD, Sorvillo F, & Mascola L., 2007). ⑧ Although media and public attention frequently focus on the intestinal illnesses of *Escherichia coli* and *Salmonella,* the mortality associated with CDI surpasses that of all other intestinal diseases combined (Redelings MD et al., 2007). ⑨ Despite scrupulous attention to hygiene measures, the incidence of CDI has continued to escalate due in part to the rise of a hypervirulent strain of *C. difficile* identified as NAP1/BI/027 toxinotype III (McDonald et al., 2005). ⑩ The NAP1/B1/027 toxinotype III pathogen is more virulent than other strains and has demonstrated resistance to common antimicrobial therapy (Kuijper, Coignard, & Tull, 2006; McDonald et al., 2005).

⑪ The financial burden associated with this disease, due to longer lengths of hospitalization and treatment, is estimated to be as high as $3.2 billon dollars annually (Dubberke et al., 2008). ⑫ Adding to this are the indirect costs of CDI, such as the pain and suffering patients will endure, which is less often acknowledged, but results in an even greater human cost. ⑬ The prevalence of CDI has particular repercussions in the elderly population where the risk of CDI can be as much as 20-fold higher than among adult patients under the age of 45 (McDonald et al., 2006). ⑭ Because nurses are at the bedside 24/7, they are positioned to impact the rate of CDI directly at the point of care. ⑮ Although not currently available, a clinical prediction rule to identify those at the greatest risk for CDI is a cost-effective, nontechnological, and nonpharmaceutical approach to translate evidence-based research into clinical bedside practice. ⑯ Operationalizing a patient's risk will enable nurses to anticipate, rather than simply react to, the increasing threat of CDI in hospitalized patients.

⑰ This proposal is the first phase in a series of studies to develop a clinical prediction rule to determine the risk of CDI in a population of surgical patients. ⑱ A clinical prediction rule, or risk score, specific for initial onset of CDI in surgical patients, to our knowledge, is without precedence in the published literature and has received only limited attention in other patient populations (Hu et al., 2008; Kyne, Sougioultzis, McFarland, & Kelly, 2002). ⑲ We propose to investigate the risk factors for CDI in a high-volume, high-risk cohort of nonemergent colectomy[12] surgical patients using data collected as part of the Michigan Surgical Quality Collaborative (MSQC). ⑳ The aims of this study are to:

1) ㉑ Determine the preoperative risk factors of colectomy patients diagnosed with CDI as compared with colectomy patients without CDI.

2) ㉒ Integrate the most robust variables associated with CDI in the postoperative colectomy patient into a clinical prediction rule model.

3) ㉓ Evaluate the predictive accuracy of the CDI prediction rule.

㉔ This proposal provides the necessary foundation for the development of a clinical prediction rule for CDI. ㉕ The broader long-term objectives of this research are to validate this preliminary evidence into a risk score for prospective clinical application and impact analysis. ㉖ We propose that the early identification of the patients most vulnerable for CDI early in, or prior to, hospitalization is the ultimate strategy to protect high-risk patients, target preventative interventions, and help curb the escalation of CDI in hospitals.

---

[12] A surgical procedure in which all or part of the large intestine is removed in order to treat or prevent disease

1. Identify the purpose of each paragraph. Does the order of information follow a pattern of organization that seems familiar?

2. Earlier we stated that research proposals should answer three questions.

   - What do you plan to do?

   - Why is this work important for the field?

   - How will you do the work?

   To what extent does this introduction do this? If these questions are not answered, what effect would this have on the proposal reviewer?

3. What language did the author use to convince the proposal reviewers that the work is important? Does the work seem important to you? Why?

4. Does the author appear to be knowledgeable? Why or why not?

5. How much background information do you think is necessary to understand the proposal? What information did the author assume the proposal reviewers would have? Was this a reasonable assumption? Why or why not?

6. Note the use of *we* in Sentences 19 and 26. Do you think the use of we is appropriate? Can you think of a way to rewrite the sentences without using the word *we?*

To understand more about the writing of the proposal, we thought it would be interesting to talk to the writer about her experience. We were curious about such things as the amount of time it took to write it, the support network underlying it, as well as mistakes made along the way. In this next task, we present our short interview with the author, Greta, as well as a few questions for you to consider.

Task Thirty-Six ▰▰▰▰▰▰▰▰▰▰▰▰▰▰▰▰▰▰▰▰▰

Take a look at this excerpt from an interview that we had with Greta, the student who wrote the proposal. Do any of her comments surprise you? Which, if any, seem relevant for the writing of a proposal in your field?

Chris: How long did it take to write the proposal?

Greta: It took a year. I had been working on it since winter term 2008 when my advisor and I decided we would be ready in April 2009.

Chris: What was the hardest part of writing the proposal?

Greta: I need to make an important distinction here: the 'proposal' versus the other parts of the grant application. The proposal is only 14 pages of the 41-page document (not including appendix). The hardest part of the proposal for me to write was the statistical portion. This is where I felt I needed some help on how to use the right wording, and my statistical methods included logistical regression, which I didn't know much about. The hardest part of the rest of the application was writing the training plan and the plan for protection of human subjects. I think what made these parts hard for me was not as much from the information, but that I was unprepared for the time it took to write these parts up. They need just as much attention and careful word-choice as the proposal.

Chris: Did you have anyone help you with it? If so, who?

Greta: "It takes a village."
- My advisor and I met once a week.
- You (Chris) and I met twice a month.
- I paid an editor to review the final copy, and she picked up some very good mistakes.
- I paid a statistician $300 to go over my power analysis/analysis up and help me with the working of my write up.
- I had several of my peers review my final proposal.
- I found it particularly helpful to look at other students' successful proposals (I had access to three), which helped me with formatting and general questions in the application.

Chris: Did you think you would get funded?

Greta: I thought I would be competitive for funding based on my topic and my preparation. I felt like I had given it my best shot.

Chris: What was your reaction to the feedback from the reviewers?

Greta: Interestingly, when I first read it, all I could see was the negative. Months later, when I read it again, I realized they really had some positive comments! And, I have actually found some of their comments and recommendations helpful. For example, one reviewer suggested that I may want to split my database—one set for the derivation cohort and one set for the validation. I may actually end up doing this.

Chris: What, if anything, would you do differently, if you could do it all again from scratch?

Greta: Ask for my letters of support much farther in advance. I got in a crunch on this because two people gave me their letters late. Luckily, I had asked for more letters than I actually needed.

Chris: Did you make any mistakes along the way that you wish you had not made?

Greta: You might be expecting something big and important here, but I did not upload my grant until two days before the proposal was due and this turned out to be a problem. Unbeknownst to me, the margins I was using did not exactly match up with the margins in the online form—even though I had set the correct margins in my document, it was not perfect. Therefore, my diagrams and tables were all in the wrong places and my document was too long. This caused me to go over the page limit by about 1/4 page. I absolutely could not cut any more from the proposal, so luckily the skilled people in our grants office stepped in and I don't know how they did it, but they crafted the document enough that they got everything to fit. Lesson learned—leave enough time for what may seem like the small stuff.

Chris: How will this success influence the writing of your next proposal?

Greta: I have been humbled because of the amount and time and support it took, not just to write the proposal, but to put all the logistics of the grant application together. I will not underestimate the skill of grantsmanship—I am not even sure that is a word, but I am using it here to mean the power of words and writing (being clear, concise and grammatically correct) to make my application stand out.

Feedback on the CDI proposal was quite positive, even though the reviewers also highlighted some weaknesses, as required by the feedback form. Several comments were made about the strength of the background section.

- Rationale and background for this work is well described. She builds on earlier work and interest in hospital safety and refines it into a focus on hospital-acquired infection.
- Applicant's research plan—to identify preoperative risk factors for *clostridium difficile* infection (CDI), and to develop and assess a clinical prediction rule—is well conceptualized and carefully laid out. The literature review was extraordinarily thorough and up to date.
- Her research could have immediate implications for addressing a critically important issue, the high and growing rate of hospital-acquired infection (HAI) in the form of CDI. I am convinced that this training will lead to an impressive program of research on patient safety.
- The background and significance sections were extraordinarily strong—in terms of developing an argument for the study, outlining a conceptual model, describing what is known to date about predictors, and outlining methodological issues involved in developing clinical prediction rules.
- Proposed area of research addresses a very large and costly problem for acutely ill, elderly surgical patients. Given the wide range of incidence (3-14%) of CDI, the very large patient pool (1,800) nested in the 23 participating hospitals may provide definitive answers about the contribution of preoperative antibiotics and bowel prep procedures to CDIs in nonemergency colon surgery patients.

Task Thirty-Seven

Based on the feedback on the background of the proposal, which of the following should be apparent in a strong proposal introduction? Place a checkmark (✓) next to the ones you are most sure about and a question mark (?) next to those you are not.

_____ 1. The rationale and background of the study are clear.

_____ 2. The author knows the relevant literature and is up-to-date.

_____ 3. The proposed research builds on earlier work and interest in the field.

_____ 4. The proposed work refines earlier work.

_____ 5. The study is well-conceptualized.

_____ 6. The research may have immediate implications.

_____ 7. The work addresses a very important issue.

_____ 8. The research offers a good solution to a problem.

Introductions to Dissertations

Dissertations can take different forms, the most common of which are traditional, article compilation, and topic based.[13] Regardless of the type, an introduction is always included. Dissertation introductions are quite challenging to write and whether these should be written before or after data collection and analysis remains open to debate. If you have done some preliminary work prior to beginning your dissertation research, this can be advantageous for the writing of your introduction since you may already have a sense that your research will yield some interesting findings and that you have reasonable questions and hypotheses to explore. If this is the case, you may have enough preliminary data to write your introduction before all of the findings are in. If, however, you have no data, you may want to delay the writing of your introduction. Recent research by Lim (2010) found that when no preliminary data is available, advisors have suggested that the best strategy is to delay writing the full introduction. Instead, you can begin by discussing the issues that led to the research, writing a little about each, and then fleshing out the introduction after the data has been analyzed.

Regardless of whether you write your introduction before or after analyzing your findings, your introduction may largely follow the CaRS model given in Table 2, but there will likely be some differences. One difference is that the different moves will be expanded, provide more detail, and may not follow the order given. Our informal research revealed that as a result of the expanded moves and details, the dissertation introductions at our institution tend to be between 10–15 pages long and contain as few as seven references to previous literature and as many as 55 (a separate literature review chapter is often included). Our research also revealed that there are disciplinary differences. For instance, dissertation introductions in education and nursing

---

[13] Traditional dissertations have separate chapters devoted to introduction, literature review (sometimes part of the introduction), methods, results, discussions, and conclusions. Article compilation dissertations consist of three or more published papers. Topic-based dissertations are organized according to research on different, but related, topics.

on average include more citations (an average of 36) than those in civil engineering, which contain on average 11 citations.[14]

Another difference between RA introductions and dissertation introductions is that the latter generally provide a rather clear indication of how the dissertation will evolve. This can be accomplished by a type of metadiscourse that Lim (2010) refers to as *directional determinants*—purpose statements, research questions, and hypotheses (if relevant for your research area)—through which you present your work.

Purpose — The purpose of this dissertation is to explore pro-social rule-breaking in the workplace, the foundation of which rests in an employee's desire to promote the welfare of his or her organization.

Research Question — Specifically, this study uses interviews to determine whether employees, when asked about their own rule-breaking behavior, would give examples that appeared to be pro-social rather than selfish or organizationally destructive.

Hypothesis — It is hypothesized that the more value one attaches to one's job or the more one cares about one's work, the more likely one will be to engage in pro-social rule breaking.

The use of directional determinants (typically associated with Move 3—presenting the present work), however, very much depends on your field of study as well as the expectations of your advisor. While dissertations in some fields such as linguistics and education may include all three types of directional determinants, in other fields such as mechanical engineering you may find only purpose statements. If all three types are present, the directional determinants should be related to each other. Specifically, your research questions reveal what you will explore within your objective, indicating the direction that you will take. The hypotheses (your expected outcomes) can be viewed as the answers to the research questions that you have posed.

---

[14] A detailed discussion of literature reviews can be found in the volume entitled *Telling a Research Story: Writing a Literature Review.*

Note how the research questions are directly related to the objectives in this excerpt from the opening paragraphs of a dissertation focusing on ethics in decision-making.

①　We make thousands of decisions in the course of a lifetime. ②　Many of these decisions not only affect our own outcomes, but also other people's outcomes. ③　As "all normal people possess a sense of morality" (Krebs, 2008, p. 149), we realize that we should pay attention to the consequences of our decisions for others. ④　But what exactly are the roles ethics and morality play in how we come to make our decisions? ⑤　When do we further our self-interest, and when do we adhere to ethical standards? ⑥　When is certain behavior perceived as ethical, and when is it not? ⑦　Moreover, how do we react when we see that ethical standards are being violated? ⑧　The aim of this dissertation is to shed more light on these questions. ⑨　More specifically, this dissertation will focus on the impact of ethics on self-interest and fairness in economic decision-making (Chapter 2 and Chapter 3), and on how we react when ethical standards are violated (Chapter 4).

⑩　This dissertation aims at providing a more comprehensive picture on when and why people behave ethically, and how they respond to people who do not maintain these standards. ⑪　To be able to tap into the underlying motives, e.g., self-interest and fairness, of ethical decision-making, I turned to the literature on economic games and game theory. ⑫　This literature provides several economic decision-making paradigms with clear and simple structures. ⑬　This makes it possible to disentangle the motivations of fairness and self-interest. ⑭　In the following part of this introduction, I will provide a short overview of the relevant literature on economic games to show how this literature can help us to study ethics in economic decision-making.

—Marijke C. Leliveld

Task Thirty-Eight

Find 3–5 dissertation introductions from your area of interest and ideally written by students of your advisor. Work through these questions to get an idea of the characteristics of dissertation introductions in your field.

1. To what extent do the introductions follow the CaRS model and include any of the variations proposed in Task Nineteen? Are any of the moves recycled or presented in a different order? About how many words are the moves? If an introduction does not follow the CaRs model, how is it organized?

2. Do the introductions contain extensive literature reviews or is the literature review a separate chapter?

3. Do the introductions contain *directional determinants*—purpose statements, research questions, and hypotheses? If so, where in the introduction do they tend to occur? To what extent are the directional determinants of elaborated? List any statements that you think are particularly nice.

4. How would you characterize the opening sentences? Do the introductions start with common knowledge? If so, what kind (facts, definitions, generalizations, something else?) A story? One of the other features described on page 19?

5. Do the introductions tend to have more integral or non-integral citations?

6. Which verbs are used to report the work of others?

7. How common are definitions? Do they seem necessary?

8. Can you detect the author's stance toward the topic? Are there any comments regarding agreement or debate in the field?

9. To what extent do the authors seem to be "present" in their texts? In other words, do you have a sense of a person behind the words in the texts?

10. In what way do think your analysis will contribute to the writing of your own introduction?

The common thread throughout this volume has been on creating contexts for your research and scholarship. To a great extent at the macro level, creating a context means moving from old work to your current work, which parallels the old to new information paradigm at the micro level, namely, the sentence. Your context is of great interest to readers, as it indicates where, in the case of an RA, the extant work stands in relation to the current discourse of the field (Charney, 1993) and, in the case of a course paper, where your thinking and knowledge stand in relation to the material to be learned. Creating a context, therefore, is central to the process of positioning yourself and your work.

References

Árvay, A., & Tankó, G. (2004). A contrastive analysis of English and Hungarian theoretical research article introductions. *IRAL, 42,* 71–100.

Anthony, L. (1999). Writing research article introductions in software engineering: How accurate is a standard model? *IEEE Transactions on Professional Communication, 42,* 38–46.

Ayers, G. (2008). The evolutionary nature of genre: An investigation of the short texts accompanying research articles in the scientific journal *Nature. English for Specific Purposes, 27*(1), 22–41.

Bazerman, C. (1985). Physicists reading physics: Schema-laden purposes and purpose-laden schema. *Written Communication, 2,* 3–24.

Bondi M. (2007). Authority and expert voices in the discourse of history. In K. Floettum, *Language and discipline perspectives on academic discourse* (pp. 66–88). Newcastle, UK: Cambridge Scholars Publishing.

Bowen, N. (2003). How to write a research article for the *Journal of Genetic Counseling. Journal of Genetic Counseling , 12*(1), 5–21.

Charles, M. (2006). Phraseological patterns in resporting clasuses used in citation: A corpus-based study of theses in two disciplines. *English for Specific Purposes, 25*(3), 310–331.

Charney, D. (1993). A study in rhetorical reading. In J. Selzer, *Understanding scientific prose* (pp. 203–231). Madison: University of Wisconsin Press.

Clark, I. (2005). *A Genre Approach to Writing Assignments.* Retrieved January 8, 2010, from Composition Forum: http://compositionforum.com/issue/14.2/clark-genre-writing.php.

Clugston, M. (2008). An analysis of citation forms in health science journals. *Journal of Academic Language and Learning, 2*(1), A11–A22.

Corbett, J. (2007). *Writing for scholarly journals: Publishing in the arts, humanities and social sciences.* Glasgow: eSharp.

Dahl, T. (2009). How economists present their knowledge claims: The linguistic representation of rhetorical function. *Written Communication, 26,* 310–391.

Duszak, A. (1997). Analyzing digressiveness in Polish academic texts. In A. Duszak, *Culture and styles of academic discourse* (pp. 323–341). Berlin: Muton de Gruyter.

Feak, C. B., Reinhart, S. M., & Sinsheimer, A. (2000). A preliminary analysis of law review notes. *English for Specific Purposes, 19*(3), 197–220.

Feak, C. B., & Swales, J. M. (2009). *Telling a research story: Writing a literature review.* Ann Arbor: University of Michigan Press.

Hartley, J. (2009). Writing an introduction to the introduction. *Journal of Technical Writing and Communication, 39*(3), 321–329.

Harwood, N. (2010). Research-based materials to demystify citation for postgraduates. In N. Harwood, *English language teaching materials: Theory and Practice* (pp. 301–321). Cambridge: Cambridge University Press.

Hyland, K. (1999). Academic attribution: Citation and the construction of disciplinary knowldege. *Applied Linguistics, 23*(3), 341–367.

Hyland, K. (2005). *Metadiscourse.* London: Continuum.

Johnson, C., & Green, B. (2009). Submitting manuscripts to biomedical journals: Common errors and helpful solutions. *Journal of Manipulative and Physiological Therapeutics, 32*(1), 1–12.

Lewin, B. A., Fine, J., & Young, L. (2001). *Expository discourse: A genre-based appropach to social science research texts.* London: Continuum.

Li, L. J., & Ge, G. C. (2009). Genre analysis: Structural and linguistic evolution of the English-medium medical research article (1985–2004). *English for Specific Purposes, 28*(2), 93–104.

Lim, J. M. H. (2010). *Schematic strategies and supervisor's expectations: A genre-based investigation into directional determinants in American doctoral dissertations on experimental language research.* Unpublished manuscript.

Motta-Roth, D. (1998). Discourse analysis and academic book reviews: A study of text and disciplinary cultures. In I. Fortanet, *Genre studies in English for academic purposes* (pp. 29–58). Castelló de la Plana: Universitat Jaume.

Neill, V. (2007). How to write a scientific masterpiece. *The Journal of Clinical Investigations, 117*(12), 35999–33602

Paul, D. (2000). Inciting chaos: A study of the rhetorical use of citations. *Journal of Business and Technical Communication, 14*, 185–222.

Samraj, B. (2002). Introductions in research articles: Variations across disciplines. *English for Specific Purposes, 21*(1), 1–17.

Shehzad, W. (2008). Move 2: establishing a niche. *Iberica, 15,* 25–49.

Skulstad, A. S. (2005). The use of metadiscourse in introductory sections of a new genre. *International Journal of Applied Linguistics, 15*(1), 71–86.

Swales, J. M. (1990). *Genre analysis: English in academic and research settings.* Cambridge: Cambridge University Press.

Swales, J. M. (2004). *Research genres: Exploration and applications.* Cambridge: Cambridge University Press.

Swales, J. M., & Feak, C. B. (2004). *Academic writing for graduate students: Essential tasks and skills,* 2nd ed. Ann Arbor: University of Michigan Press.

Thompson, G. (2001). Interaction in academic writing: Learning to argue with the reader. *Applied Linguistics, 22*(1), 58–78.

Thompson, G., & Ye, Y. (1991). Evaluation in the reporting verbs used in academic papers. *Applied Linguistics, 12*(4), 365–382.

Thompson, P. (2000). Citation practices in PhD theses. In L. Burnard, & T. McEnery, *Rethinking language pedagogy from a corpus perspective.* Frankfurt: Peter Lang.

Thompson, P., & Tribble, C. (2001). Looking at citations: Using corpora in English for academic purposes. *Language Learning & Technology, 5*(3), 91–105.

Tucker, P. (2003). Evaluation in the art-historical research article. *Journal of English for Academic Purposes, 2*(4), 291–312.

Winsor, D. (1993). Owning corporate texts. Journal of Business and Technical Communication, *7,* 179–195.